Funny Stuff

Over 400 clean jokes
you can tell your grandma

Clyde Murdock

BARBOUR
PUBLISHING, INC.
Uhrichsville, Ohio

Funny Stuff

We wish to acknowledge the following for granting permission to quote from their material:

Broadman Press, Nashville, TN for anecdotes taken from *The Treasury of Clean Jokes* by Tal Bonham. Copyright 1986 Broadman Press. All rights reserved. Used by permission.

Zondervan Publishing House, Grand Rapids, MI for anecdotes from *A Treasury of Humor* by Clyde Murdock.

Dolphin Books, Doubleday & Company, Inc., Garden City, NY for anecdotes from *3500 Good Jokes for Speakers* by Jerry Lieberman.

Regency Books for anecdotes taken from *1001 Very Clean Jokes for Every Occasion* by Bruce Wade.

Kregel Publications, Grand Rapids, MI for anecdotes taken from *The Sourcebook of Family Humor* by Oren Arnold.

Arthur Tonne, Marion, KS for anecdotes taken from *Jokes Priests Can Tell*.

Published by Barbour Publishing, Inc., P.O. Box 719, Uhrichsville, Ohio 44683 http://www.barbourbooks.com

Printed in the United States of America.

Contents

Funny Business 7

Funny Farmers 29

Funny Friendships 35

Gags about Golf 43

Hilarity in the Hereafter 49

Kidding the Congregation 61

Kidding the Kindred 71

Kidding the Kids 101

Laughing at Lawyers 111

Laughing with Legislators 117

Marital Mirth 123

Medical Mirth 133

Ministerial Mirth 145

Miscellaneous Mirth 177

Ribbing the Retired 217

Funny Business

Funny Business

On a trip through the hill country, a motorist stopped at a small crossroads store for a soft drink. The proprietor, who had been resting comfortably in a rocker on the front porch, got up and followed the customer inside. He said he had soft drinks in the quart size only, and that they were a dollar a bottle.

"But isn't that a little high?" asked the man.

"Well," replied the storekeeper, "I had to get up to wait on you."

"But you won't get many more customers at that price, will you?"

The proprietor grinned and said, "Won't need any."

◆

Some fellow held up a bank and shoved a note to the teller that said, "This is a stickup! Hand over your cash."

She shoved a note back to him that read, "Straighten your tie, stupid. We're taking your picture."

◆

The IRS has streamlined its tax form this year to read:

A. How much did you make last year?

B. How much do you have left?

C. Send B.

Funny Stuff

A definition of inflation: What used to cost five dollars to buy now costs ten dollars to repair.

The shy employee asked for Thursday off so he and his wife could celebrate their twenty-fifth wedding anniversary. His boss said, "It's okay this time but I don't intend to put up with this every twenty-five years."

Two shrewd business partners bought a special lot of suits. In the lot was a purple one, which they couldn't sell.

One of the partners became so angry about the purple suit, he went home. "I won't be back until you sell it," he said furiously, slamming the door behind him.

His partner called him at home in a couple of hours and said, "Come on back. I sold it."

Returning to the store and finding his partner scratched, cut and bleeding, he inquired, "What's the matter? Did you have to fight the customer to sell it?"

"No, but I had quite a time with his seeing eye dog."

Funny Business

A millionaire was asked how he got rich.

"Well," he said, "I began by buying peanuts for five cents a bag and selling them for ten cents. I worked long hours and all holidays. However, I didn't become a millionaire for another five years."

"What happened?" his interviewer asked.

"Well, then my father died and left me a chain of hotels."

Two Texas oilmen walked into a Cadillac car agency and priced a top of the line model. "That one sells for $44,695.92," said the salesman.

"I'll just take it," said the first Texan as he reached for his checkbook.

The other Texan grabbed his hand and said, "No, let me get it. You bought lunch today."

The furious customer called the waitress over to his table and demanded to know what was in his soup.

She looked and shyly said, "I'll have to call the boss; I don't know one insect from another."

Funny Stuff

A salesman, applying for a new job, claimed to be the greatest salesman in the world. The firm hired him.

At the end of the first day the fellow dejectedly came back to his office. "I am not the world's greatest salesman after all," he said. "The greatest salesman is the man who loaded you up with this stuff you want me to sell."

◆

An unethical housepainter painted a Baptist church. He thinned the paint until it was like water.

After he had finished painting the church, there came a torrential rainstorm that washed all the thin paint off.

Then suddenly the sun came out brightly and a voice out of the sky said to the painter, "Repent. Repaint. And go and thin no more."

◆

A businessman on his deathbed called his friend and said, "Bill, I want you to promise me that when I die you will have my remains cremated."

"And what," his friend asked, "do you want me to do with your ashes?"

The businessman said, "Just put them in an envelope and mail them to the Internal Revenue Service and write on the envelope, 'Now you have everything.'"

Funny Business

The agent who led his company with persistency in life insurance sales made up his mind he was going to marry the company vice president's daughter. She didn't like the guy at all, but he knew how to be persistent.

He began an extensive direct mail campaign, supplemented by several phone calls and face-to-face interviews. Soon, he stepped up his direct mail program, sending her a special delivery letter for forty-seven days. On the forty-eighth day, his persistence produced results.

She married the mailman.

A fellow who owned a pizza shop was audited by the IRS.

The agent said, "I want to know about all of your travel expenses. For example, you have expenses for six trips to Rome just this year. How do you justify this?"

"Justify nothing. Don't you know? We deliver!"

Funny Stuff

The IRS was baffled by a letter from a man who explained that he hadn't been able to sleep well since 1970 when he cheated on his income tax. Enclosed in the letter were five $100 bills.

The man concluded the letter by saying that if he didn't sleep better now, he would send the rest.

Teacher: "Boys and girls, there is a wonderful example in the life of the ant. Every day the ant goes to work and works all day. Every day the ant is busy. And in the end, what happens?"

Johnny: "Someone steps on him."

The customer wanted to buy a chicken and the butcher had only one in stock. He weighed it and said, "A beauty. That will be $1.25."

"Oh, that's not quite large enough," said the customer. The butcher put the chicken back in the refrigerator, rolled it around on the ice several times—then back on the scales again.

"This one is $1.85," he said, adding his thumb to the weight.

"Oh, that's fine!" said the customer. "I'll take both of them."

Funny Business

A retail store owner wired a manufacturer for a consignment of goods and by return wire received the following message: "We can't ship your goods until you pay for the last consignment."

The store owner wired back: "Cancel that new order. I can't wait that long!"

A minister was telling the banker about the new choir director.

"He has a marvelous voice," he said. "He can hold a note for two minutes."

"That's nothing," said the banker. "I have held one of his notes for two years!"

A tailor decided to mail order a gizmo that's used to press sleeves called a "tailor's goose." Sitting down to write his letter he realized he needed two of them. So he wrote: "Please send me two tailor's gooses."

But that didn't sound exactly right, so he tore it up and began all over again: "Please send me two tailor's geese."

That didn't sound right either, so again he tore up his letter and wrote: "Please send me one tailor's goose. P.S. Please send me another one, too."

A motorist got stuck in a mud hole in the country.

A farmer was there with his tractor and pulled him out for fifty dollars.

"At these prices, I would think you would be pulling people out day and night," the motorist said.

"Can't. At night I haul water for the hole."

✦

A man applying for a job asked the interviewer whether the company paid the hospital insurance. The interviewer explained that the worker would have to pay for it, but it would be deducted from his check.

"The last place I worked for the company paid for it," the man interjected.

"Did they pay for your life insurance too?" the interviewer asked.

"Sure, they did," was the answer. "Not only that, but we got unlimited sick leave, severance pay, three weeks vacation, a holiday bonus, coffee breaks. . ."

"Then why did you leave such a perfect place?" the interviewer asked.

"The company folded," the man replied.

An old miner, because of his exceptional thrift, had no friends. Just before he died, he called his doctor, lawyer, and minister together around his bedside.

"I have always heard that you can't take it with you, but I am going to prove you can," he said. "I've put $30,000 in each of these three envelopes. When I pass on I want each of you to take an envelope and just before they throw the dirt on me, you throw your envelope in."

The three attended the funeral and each threw his envelope in the grave. On the way back from the cemetery the minister said, "I just don't feel exactly right. My conscience hurts me. I'm going to confess. I needed $10,000 badly for a new church we are building, so I took out $10,000 and threw the $20,000 in the grave."

The doctor said, "I too, must confess. I am building a hospital and I took $20,000 and threw in only $10,000."

The lawyer said, "Gentlemen, I'm surprised, shocked, and ashamed of you. I don't see how you could hold out like this. I threw in my personal check for the full amount."

An American skiing in Switzerland got separated from his group and fell, uninjured, into a deep crevasse. Several hours later, a rescue party found the yawning pit, and to reassure the stranded skier, shouted down to him, "We're from the Red Cross!"

"Sorry," the American echoed back, "I already gave at the office!"

◆

A modern Rip Van Winkle slept for twenty years. When he awakened, he called his stockbroker and said, "How did the market do in the past twenty years?"

"Oh, great," his broker exclaimed, offering the following breakdown:

—100 shares, AT&T—nine million dollars

—100 shares, GE—eight million

—100 shares, General Motors—nineteen million

"Great," Rip cried. "I'm rich."

At that point the telephone operator interrupted, "Your three minutes are up, sir. Please deposit a million dollars."

◆

I have nothing against the income tax. It's just that every time my ship comes in, the government unloads it.

Funny Business

The airline company was disturbed over the high percentage of accidents and decided to eliminate human errors by building a completely mechanical plane.

"Ladies and gentlemen," came a voice over the loudspeaker on the maiden voyage, "it may interest you to know that you are now traveling in the world's first completely automatic plane. Now just sit back and relax for nothing can go wrong. . .go wrong. . .go wrong. . . !"

✦

A young fellow walked into the automobile show-room and pointed to a really sporty model.

"If I bought this car by installments, how long would it take me to pay for it?" he inquired.

"That would depend on how much you could afford each month, sir," replied the salesman cautiously.

The young man scratched his chin. "Well, I think I could manage three dollars a month."

"Three dollars a month!" gasped the salesman. "At that rate, it would take a hundred years."

Looking fondly at the auto, the young man replied, "It's a bargain at that. I'll take it."

Funny Stuff

A sausage manufacturer made a reputation for a certain brand of sausage. He called it rabbit sausage. A sanitary inspector called one day to make an analysis.

"Don't you use some horse meat in making this sausage?" asked the inspector.

"Yes, I use some," was the reply.

"How much?"

"Well, I make it a fifty-fifty proposition. One horse and one rabbit."

✦

A professor's chauffeur told him, "You make $40,000 a year and I only make $5,000 a year and I can deliver your twenty-minute lecture as well as you can."

"Oh, you can, can you? Well, you make my next speech at the college."

The chauffeur got up to speak and after he had finished the leader said, "We now have a question period."

A tall fellow stood and said "Sir, tell me the age of the dinosaurs and the name of the rock under which they are buried."

The chauffeur said, "That is such a ridiculous question, that I'm going to ask my chauffeur to answer it."

An angry lady went into a grocery store and told a clerk that she wanted one-half head of lettuce and she wanted it now. "Get going!" she screamed.

"But lady," the young man meekly said, "we don't have half heads of lettuce."

"Young man," she shrieked, "get a knife and cut a head in two."

"Yes ma'am," he said. "Let me go back and talk to the manager."

He found the manager and said, "There's a crabby woman out there who wants one-half head of lettuce."

He suddenly glanced over his shoulder and there stood the woman.

He quickly said, "And here is the nice lady who wants the other half."

◆

One executive was telling another about the trouble he had in keeping a secretary.

"I lost the last one," he said, "because we had so many coffee breaks that she couldn't sleep nights."

◆

A fellow made the following New Year's resolution: "I have made up my mind to live within my means, and I'm going to keep this promise if I have to borrow money to do it."

Funny Stuff

A Texan plunked down a $500 bill on the airplane counter and said, "Give me a ticket."

"Where do you want to go?" asked the clerk.

"Oh, anywhere. I've got businesses everywhere," he replied.

◆

The manager of the Wild West Railroad wrote the overseer a letter.

He wrote, "Don't be so long-winded in your reports. Write a business letter, not a love letter."

A few days later, the railroad line was badly flooded and the overseer wrote the manager his report.

He wrote, "Sir, where the railroad was, the river is."

◆

The manager of a restaurant called his waitresses together. "Girls," he began, "I want you all to look your best today. Greet every customer with a smile, put on a little extra makeup, and see to it that your hair is in place."

"What's up?" asked one of the girls. "Bunch of big shots coming in today?"

"No," explained the manager, "the meat's tough today."

Funny Business

Salesman: "I've been trying to see you for a week. When may I have an appointment?"

Executive: "Make a date with my secretary."

Salesman: "I did, and we had a swell time, but I still want to see you."

✦

Customer: "I hear my son has owed you for a suit for three years."

Tailor: "Yes, sir. Have you called to settle the account?"

Customer: "No, I'd like one for myself on the same terms."

✦

It was a chance meeting of two young men who had been boyhood friends.

"Do you know that I've taken up writing as a career?"

"Wonderful! Have you sold anything yet?"

"Yes, my watch, my television set, and my car!"

✦

A wealthy man cashed a huge personal check which came back from the bank with "Insufficient Funds" stamped across the face.

Beneath the stamped words was the hand-written notation: "Not you, us."

Funny Stuff

A man was a great worrier, always burdened down with his brow wrinkled, and never a smile on his face.

One day he became very happy, bouncing along with a big smile on his face, and victory in his voice.

A friend said, "My goodness, what has changed you?"

He said, "I have quit worrying. I have found a professional worrier that I have hired to do all my worrying for me."

His friend said, "Great, but what does it cost you?"

"I pay $1,000 a week," he replied.

His friend said, "Man, that's a lot of money. You don't have that kind of money. How are you going to pay that?"

He said, "Oh, that's his worry."

A Texan on the plane began bragging of the property he owned.

"How much property do you own?" asked the man seated next to him.

"Thirty acres," answered the Texan.

"That doesn't sound like much for a Texan," said the other fellow.

"Downtown Dallas."

24

Funny Business

A big company executive attended a United Fund meeting and pledged one hundred percent cooperation from all his employees.

After the meeting, he returned to his company and instructed his manager to collect a contribution from all his employees as he had promised.

After three days the manager reported that all had given with the exception of John Jones who refused to give in spite of all his persuading.

"Have him come to my office," the big executive instructed.

"Jones, I hear that you have refused to contribute to the United Fund," the executive said.

"Yes, sir," replied John Jones. "I never do give to it."

"Jones, I have promised that all will contribute and you will either do so or be fired," thundered the chief.

John Jones meekly took out his billfold and laid a fifty-dollar bill on the executive's desk.

"I would have given it sooner but nobody ever explained it the way you just did," he added.

◆

Patron in shoe repair shop: "I found this ticket
    from 1977. I don't reckon you still have them."
Cobbler: "They'll be ready on Friday."

The president of a large corporation was chairing a meeting of his board of directors. He had a plan which he knew some directors did not favor. He presented his plan and then declared: "All in favor of this plan please reply by saying 'Aye.' All opposed reply by saying 'I resign.' "

◆

One day the boss asked one of the workers: "Bill, do you believe in life after death?"

Bill replied: "Sure do, boss. Why do you ask?"

"Well," answered the boss, "the other morning you asked for time off for your grandmother's funeral. That same afternoon she came in looking for you."

◆

A woman telephoned the owner of a store at three o'clock in the morning. "I want to tell you how beautiful the table is I bought from your store four months ago!"

"Thank you, but why call me at three in the morning to tell me when you bought it four months ago?"

"It just arrived!"

Funny Business

A young man rushed into a service station to use the telephone. "Sir, do you have need of a young boy to work for you?" he was heard to inquire. "You don't! You've already got a good boy? Thank you, sir."

With that he hung up the receiver and started to leave, whistling merrily.

The attendant was surprised. "Why are you whistling after you heard they already have a good boy and don't need you? What makes you so happy?"

"Well," said the boy, "I'm the good boy that they've got, and I was just checking on my job."

✦

A worker was stealing from the farm where he worked. Every day the foreman would punch the straw in the wheelbarrow. "I know you are stealing, but I can never find out what," he would say.

The foreman was transferred to another farm. He said to the worker, "I know you are stealing something and I am being transferred and can't get you fired. Tell me what it is."

"Wheelbarrows," he replied.

Funny Farmers

Funny Farmers

A farmer had a very sick mule, so he called the veterinarian. The vet took his little black bag and, upon arrival, took the mule's pulse, temperature, and all the things that you do when you examine a sick mule.

The vet said, "This is a very sick mule, and I want you to give it these little white pills immediately. These white ones are very potent, and will cure practically anything a sick mule has. But just to be sure, wait four hours and give the mule one of these red pills. They are so strong, they will cure anything."

The farmer and doctor met in about two weeks, and the doctor asked the farmer what happened to the mule.

"Well, I gave him the white pills like you told me, doc. And I never saw so much reaction from one mule in all my life. He kicked down the barn door, tore through the back fence, and took off across the country. I thought I had lost my mule."

"Did you lose him?" the doctor asked.

"You know, Doc, if I hadn't had the presence of mind to take that red pill, that mule would have been long gone."

Funny Stuff

A young man joined the Peace Corps and was sent to help on a farm. He watched the farmer milk one cow and asked the farmer to let him take over milking the other one.

Sometime later the farmer returned to the barn, just in time to see the young man feeding the milk back to the cow.

"What in the world are you doing that for?" asked the farmer.

The young man explained, "Well, the milk looked a little thin, so I thought I'd run it back through again."

◆

A man in the country saw a three-legged chicken. It ran beside the car, and finally passed him like a flash.

He stopped at a farmer's house and said, "I just saw a three-legged chicken."

"Yes," said the farmer, "we have a yard full of them."

"Why do you have three-legged chickens?" the man asked.

"We all like drumsticks and we have three in our family," said the farmer.

"Well, how do they taste?" asked the traveler.

"How do I know? We never caught one."

Funny Farmers

An old farmer needed a bank loan badly, for his crops had failed, his wife was sick, and his son was put out of school.

But he made a mistake by taking his dog with him when he went to the bank.

You know how bankers are, when you need a loan, hard to get along with.

Now the old dog was generally gentle, but in the bank he got aggravated and jumped up and bit the banker. Then on the way out he bit two patrons of the bank.

Of course, the next scene was the courtroom.

The judge said, "Farmer, why did you bring this vicious dog in this bank?"

The farmer said, "Judge, he ain't vicious."

"Then why did he bite three people?" the judge asked.

The farmer replied, "I don't know why he bit the banker, but I do know why he bit the other two people."

"Why?" asked the judge.

"To get the bad taste out of his mouth," he replied.

Funny Friendships

Funny Friendships

A neighbor telephoned his neighbor at three o'clock in the morning, and said, "Your dog is barking and keeping me awake."

The other neighbor called him back at 3 A.M. the next day, and said, "I don't have a dog."

Two old friends met one day after many years. One had attended college, and now was very successful. The other had not attended college and never had much ambition.

The successful one said, "How has everything been going with you?"

"Well, one day I opened the Bible at random, and dropped my finger on a word and it was oil. So, I invested in oil, and boy, did the oil wells gush. Then another day I dropped my finger on another word and it was gold. So, I invested in gold and those mines really produced. Now, I'm as rich as Rockefeller."

The successful friend was so impressed that he rushed to his hotel, grabbed a Gideon Bible, flipped it open, and dropped his finger on a page.

He opened his eyes and his finger rested on the words "Chapter Eleven."

Two friends went hunting for moose in Canada each year.

Each time they were flown out to the marshland in a small bush airplane.

After landing them at the hunting site, the pilot said, "I'll pick you up in four days, and you can only return with you two, your gear, and only one moose."

In four days when the pilot landed to pick them up he found the men with two moose. He was furious. "I told you only one moose. It's impossible to fly out with the weight of two."

The men said, "But we were here last year and that pilot took us with two moose, so we thought maybe you would too."

The pilot said, "I'm the best pilot in this country, so if he can do it, I can too."

So they stuffed everything in the small plane, closed the door, and took off. He pulled the throttle down as far as it would go.

They made it up fine, until they came to a tree at the end of the runway and suddenly crashed right in the top of it.

Moose, gear, and men went in all directions. When one of the hunters came to, he looked around and said, "Herb, where are we?"

The other said, "I don't know, Bill, but it's about 150 yards farther than we were last year."

Funny Friendships

A cheapskate was shopping for an inexpensive birthday gift for his friend. The only thing he could find in his price range was a badly broken vase. He bought it for almost nothing and asked the store to ship it, figuring his friend would think it was broken in the mail. A week later he received a note: "Many thanks for the vase. It was nice of you to wrap each piece separately."

Fred Abernathy always read the obituary column of the daily paper. All of Fred's friends knew of this habit. One day they decided to play a trick on him by placing his name and picture in the obituaries.

The following morning Fred picked up his newspaper, turned to the obituary page, and there he saw his name, his biography, and his photo.

Startled, he went to the telephone and rang up his pal, George. "Listen," he said. "Do you have the morning paper? You do? Please turn to the obituary page. What do you see in the second column?"

There was a pause, then George said, "Holy smokes! It's you, Fred! It's you all right! Listen, where are you calling from?"

Man (with hands over the eyes of the woman): "If you can't guess who it is in three guesses, I'm going to kiss you."

Woman: "Jack Frost, Santa Claus, and Christopher Columbus."

◆

This afternoon tea has been a brilliant affair, thought the hostess as she made the rounds checking on the wants of her guests.

Then she spotted the guest of honor seated in a chair far removed from the other guests.

"Are you enjoying yourself?" asked the hostess.

"Yes," replied the gentleman, "but that's all I'm enjoying."

◆

"Hello, Hello. . . Is that you, Sam?"

"Yeah, this is Sam."

"It doesn't sound like Sam."

"This is Sam."

"Are you sure this is Sam?"

"Certainly, this is Sam."

"Well, listen, Sam. This is Bill. Lend me fifty dollars."

"All right. I'll tell Sam when he comes in."

Funny Friendships

A man asked his friend if he could keep a secret. "What is your secret?" his friend asked.

"I need to borrow some money," he replied.

"Don't worry, my friend," his friend replied. "It's as if I had never heard it."

A woman had been bitten by a mad dog and looked as if she were doing to die. The doctor told her she had better make her will. Taking her pen and paper she began to write. In fact, she wrote and wrote.

Finally, the doctor said, "This is surely a lengthy will you are making."

"Will, nothing," she raved. "I'm making a list of all the people I'm going to bite."

Mrs. Watson and Mrs. Hale met one morning while sweeping their front walks. "You are looking mighty nice this morning, "ventured Mrs. Watson.

Mrs. Hale sniffed and said, "I regret that I could not say as much about you."

Mrs. Watson shot right back, "If you were as big a liar as I am, you could."

Funny Stuff

There were two friends, one thin and the other fat. They met one day and the fat one said, "You look like you've been in a famine."

"Yes," replied the thin man, "and you look like you caused it!"

◆

One friend says to the other, "Look, we've been friends for a long time. I know what you're losing on the market. Tell me—this has to affect your sleep—how do you sleep at night?"

The other says, "I sleep like a baby."

"What do you mean you sleep like a baby?"

"I wake up every two hours and cry."

Gags
about
Golf

Gags about Golf

A golfer came home from a hard eighteen-hole golf match with some of his neighbors.

His wife greeted him and said, "Well, honey, did you win the game today?"

"Well," he said, "let's put it this way. I got to hit the ball more times than anyone else."

An inept golfer drove his tee shot onto an anthill. After many swings he had demolished the anthill, but still had not hit the ball. At this point one of the two ants still alive turned to the other and said, "If we want to stay alive, we'd better get on the ball."

Harry, who was eighty-three, shot a great game of golf, but his eyesight was going and he couldn't see where he hit the ball. He was advised to take Sam with him. Sam could no longer hit the ball, but his eyes were perfect. Harry hit the ball and turned to Sam to ask, "Did you see where the ball went?"

Sam said, "Exactly."

"Where is it?" asked Harry.

"I forget," Sam answered.

A golfer teed off and accidentally hit a bystander on the head. Enraged, the bystander yelled, "I am going to sue you for $5000."

The golfer replied, "I said 'fore.' "

The bystander answered, "Okay, I'll take it."

✦

A fellow came home from a golf game one day, and his neighbor asked him how he had done.

"I shot seventy," the golfer replied.

The neighbor said, "Man, that's great."

The golfer said, "Yeah, and tomorrow I'll play the second hole."

✦

A golfer was playing a hole that had to be shot over water.

He, like all of us, got out an old ball and teed up.

A voice out of nowhere said, "Use a new ball."

He didn't see anybody, but he put a new ball on the tee, and was ready to hit the ball when the voice said, "Take a practice swing."

He took a practice swing, and the voice said, "Use the old ball."

Gags about Golf

A golfer shot a ball on a short hole, and it rolled very near the hole.

Another man was putting on the same hole, but he couldn't see the man who had shot the ball because of a hill.

The man who had shot the ball came near the hole and the man who was putting decided to make the old boy happy, so he pushed his ball in the cup. He said, "Friend, look in the cup and get a big surprise."

The player lifted the ball and yelled to his partner, who was coming over the hill, "Hey, Joe, how about that? I sank it for a nine."

Hilarity in the Hereafter

Three men died and went to heaven.

Saint Peter asked, "Why should I let you in? What did you do to earn your entrance?"

One man said, "I was a policeman, and I helped a lot of people."

The second man said, "I was a nurse, and I helped a lot of people."

Saint Peter said, "Go right on in."

The third man said, "I was an executive on the HMO and I got a lot of people out of the hospital real soon."

Saint Peter said, "Go right on in, but you can stay for only two days."

✦

Three blind mice went to heaven, and Saint Peter asked how they liked it.

"Oh, it's good, but it's so large, it takes too long to get anywhere," they replied.

He gave them each a pair of roller skates and they skated all around heaven.

Later, a cat went to heaven. Saint Peter asked, "How do you like it up here?"

"Oh, it's great—especially those meals on wheels," the cat replied.

A young man fell into a coma, but recovered before his friends had buried him. One of them asked what it felt like to be dead.

"Dead!" he exclaimed. "I wasn't dead. And I knew I wasn't, because my feet were cold and I was hungry."

"But how did that make you sure?"

"Well, I knew that if I were in heaven, I shouldn't be hungry, and if I was in the other place, my feet wouldn't be cold."

◆

A man found the angels in heaven so bland, the music so terrible, and the food so monotonous that he went for a week's visit to hell.

He had a swinging time down there with gourmet food, hot jazz, and beautiful ladies, so at the end of his visit he asked Saint Peter for a permanent transfer.

But when he returned to hell there were no available gals, the music was shrieking, the food was sickening, and there were little glowing red workers always sticking hot pokers and pitchforks in him. When he complained, the devil explained: "Last week you were a tourist. Now you're an immigrant."

"How's your wife?" a fellow asked his old friend.

"She's in heaven," replied the friend.

"Oh, I'm sorry," the fellow answered. Then realizing that was not the best phrase to use, he said, "I mean, I'm glad. . .well, what I really mean is, I'm surprised."

◆

Three women, one Jewish, one Catholic, and one Baptist, died and went to heaven.

Saint Peter asked the Catholic, "What have you brought with you to heaven?" She replied, "I brought the rosary."

He asked the Jewish woman what she brought and she replied, "I brought the Star of David."

Then he asked the Baptist what she brought and she said, "I brought a covered dish."

◆

A funeral happened to pass by an armored truck at an intersection. Since the truck could not get through the procession, the driver pulled out and joined it.

An onlooker saw the armored truck in the funeral procession and remarked to a friend, "What do you know? You can take it with you."

A man died and went to heaven. Saint Peter said, "You must be able to spell a word before I can let you enter."

"What is the word?"

Saint Peter said, "Love. You can spell that, can't you?"

"Sure. L-O-V-E."

Saint Peter said, "Good, go right on in."

Just then Peter was called away to the telephone. He said to the man, "You mind the gate while I'm gone and remember, if anyone comes he or she must spell the word."

A few minutes later the man's wife knocked on the gate.

"What in the world are you doing here?" he asked.

She said, "After your elaborate funeral, I was in a car wreck. So, here I am."

He said, "Fine, but Saint Peter said that you must be able to spell a word before I can let you in."

"That's okay. What's the word?"

He replied, "Czechoslovakia."

Hilarity in the Hereafter

Jeff and Murray loved baseball. They ate, drank, and slept the game. One day over lunch, Jeff said, "Wouldn't it be awful if when we died there weren't any baseball in heaven?"

"Oh, that would be the pits," replied Murray. "Tell you what—whoever dies first, let's make a pact he comes back and somehow lets the other guy know if there's any baseball."

"You got it!"

Six months later, Murray passed away and Jeff was heartbroken.

One summer morning, he was walking along the street when he felt a tap on his shoulder. He turned but no one was there.

"It's me, your old pal," said a voice.

"Is that you, Murray?"

"Yeah," said the voice. "Just the way we made our pact, I've come back."

"Tell me, buddy, is there baseball in heaven?"

"Well, there's a good side to it and a bad side. The good news is there's a baseball game every day. Ruth and Gehrig can still hit the ball a mile. Now here's the bad news. You're pitching this Friday."

Funny Stuff

A man rushed in the First Denominational Church and asked to use the phone. He noticed two phones, one green and one red. He asked what was the difference in the two colors. He was told that the green one was for all local calls, and the red one was a direct line to heaven.

"I'd like to talk to the Lord. How much does it cost on the red phone?" The man answered, "It will cost you a thousand dollars."

Later that day he visited the Second Denominational Church and noticed the same phones, green and red. He asked "What is the red phone for?"

"Oh, it's a direct line to heaven," he was told. "How much does it cost?" he asked. "Twenty-five cents," was the reply.

"Why so cheap?" he asked.

"Well, you see," the pastor replied, "it's only a local call at our church."

A local newspaper had a very difficult time in reporting the death of one of the town members.

The first report said, "Brother Smith has gone to rust."

They tried to correct the misprint the next day and it came out, "Brother Smith has gone to roost."

Finally, they tried a third time and the report stated, "Brother Smith has gone to roast."

A politician went to heaven, and was put at the front of the line.

Some said to Saint Peter, "Why did you let this guy go to the front of the line? After all, we have pastors, evangelists, and Sunday school teachers up here."

Saint Peter said, "Yes, I know, but we only have one politician up here."

◆

A neighbor brought her new four-month-old baby to visit her neighbor. The baby soon began to fuss.

The son of the neighbor she visited said, "Where did you get him?"

"He was sent from heaven," the mother replied.

As the infant continued to cry and yell, the little boy said, "I bet I know why he was sent from heaven. God wanted it quiet up there!"

◆

Saint Peter and Saint John were playing golf in heaven.

Saint John, on the first hole, drove a long shot, approached the green on the second shot, and dropped the ball in the cup for a three.

Saint Peter drove the green and the ball rolled in the cup for a hole in one.

Saint John said very sternly, "Now, Peter, stop those miracles and get along with the game."

A rich woman died and went to heaven.

There she saw her maid riding in a Rolls Royce to a big mansion.

She thought, *If my maid gets all of this treatment, I can't wait to see what I will get.*

But was she surprised when Saint Peter gave her a bicycle. She couldn't believe it and became very gloomy.

However, later Saint Peter noticed she was happy again.

"Why are you so happy with your bicycle?" he asked.

She replied, "I just saw my pastor go by on roller skates."

◆

A nagging wife was always scolding her husband on every occasion.

One day she died. At the graveside service, suddenly there was a great clap of thunder and a big bolt of lightning streaked across the sky.

The bereaved husband contemplated this for a few seconds.

Then finally he turned to the minister and said, "Reverend, I think she made it."

Hilarity in the Hereafter

Determined to "take it with him" when he died, a very rich man prayed until finally the Lord gave in. There was one condition: he could bring only one suitcase of his wealth. The rich man decided to fill the case with gold bullion.

The day came when God called him home. Saint Peter greeted him, but told him he couldn't bring his suitcase. "Oh, but I have an agreement with God," the man explained.

"That's unusual," said Saint Peter. "Mind if I take a look?" The man opened the suitcase to reveal the shining gold bullion.

Saint Peter was amazed. "Why in the world would you bring pavement?"

Kidding the Congregation

Kidding the Congregation

A small church in the hills of Tennessee struck oil on its parking lot. It was a gusher and money was coming in so fast the finance committee didn't know what to do with it.

The committee called a special congregational meeting of the forty members of the church and asked what to do with all the money.

Deacon Brown said, "I move that we divide all the money among our forty members, and I further move that we don't take in any new members."

✦

One day an old mountain deacon was caught in the alley, taking a little drink.

A fellow deacon said, "You know you ought not to do that. . .you know the Lord will see you."

"Yes, Brother Deacon, but He ain't a big blabbermouth like a lot of people I know."

✦

A church had a great Sunday service.

The next Sunday one of the deacons prayed, "Lord, the last morning service was so great. It was wonderful, just unbelievable. Lord, You should have been there."

A country preacher was preaching very pointedly to his congregation one Sunday night.

He said, "Now let the church walk."

Deacon Jones said, "Amen, let it walk."

The preacher then said, "Let the church run."

Deacon Jones said, "Amen, parson, let it run."

"Let the church fly," said the preacher.

"Amen, brother, let it fly," said Deacon Jones.

"Now it's going to take money to let it fly, brother."

"Let it walk," said Deacon Jones. "Let it walk."

✦

An elderly lady attended a church after a rather long absence. She noticed a bronze plaque in the vestibule of the church, and after the service asked the minister what it was.

He explained that it was a memorial to the men who had been in the services.

"What are the dates beside some of the names?" she asked.

"Those are the ones who died in the service," replied the minister.

"Which one, pastor, the 9:30 or 11:00 o'clock service?"

Kidding the Congregation

A preacher was addressing the people one Sunday, trying to impress upon them the importance of religion. "All you people of this congregation," he cried from the pulpit, "one day you're going to die. Do you hear me? All you people of this congregation, one day you're going to die."

One little man sitting in the front pew started to laugh, so the preacher asked him, "What's so funny?"

The man answered, "I don't belong to this congregation."

◆

At the Sunday dinner table a lady asked her husband, "Did you notice the mink coat on the lady in front of us in church today?"

"No," admitted the husband, "I was dozing."

"Huh," retorted the wife, "a lot of good the sermon did you."

◆

A man was asked to lead the congregational singing.

"I can't do it," he replied. "The last time I tried, the piano player said she played on all the black keys—and on all the white keys—and I still sang in the cracks."

Funny Stuff

A visitor to a drought-stricken area was engaged in conversation at the local store about the no-rain situation.

"You think the drought is bad here," the merchant observed. "But down south of here a ways, they haven't had any for so long that the Baptists are sprinkling, the Methodists are using a damp cloth, and the Presbyterians are issuing rain checks!"

✦

A woman went into a small town post office and asked for five dollars worth of stamps.

"What denomination?" asked the clerk.

"Well," came the angry reply, "I didn't know it would ever come to this, but if you must know, I'm a Methodist!"

✦

The church member was delinquent in paying his pledge, and the matter was referred to the minister.

"You are a respectable citizen," the minister chided. "You always pay your debts to everyone else. Why not pay your debts to the Lord?"

"Well, to tell you the truth," the member answered, "He just doesn't push as hard as some of the others."

Kidding the Congregation

A church convention of over a thousand delegates met for a week in a certain city.

"I suppose business is good, with all these delegates here," a regular customer mentioned to one of the storekeepers.

Lamented the storekeeper: "They came with the Ten Commandments in one hand, a ten-dollar bill in the other hand, and they haven't broken either one of them yet."

An aged couple was listening to a broadcast church service. Both sat in deep contemplation, and half an hour went by. Then suddenly the old man burst into a fit of laughter.

"Sandy," exclaimed his wife in a horrified tone, "why this merriment on the Sabbath?"

"Ah," said Sandy, "the preacher's just announced the offering, and here I am safe at home."

The pastor's son, who didn't know any curse words, was up against it when a cantankerous kid next door gave him so much trouble.

He said in anger, "Oh you—you—you board member!"

A race track operator offered a gift to a church for its building fund.

The church held a business meeting to decide if they could accept it.

The pastor asked the board, "Should we accept this gift from the race track or not?"

One member spoke up and said, "I don't see why we don't accept his money. He always accepts mine."

The soloist was singing in a high-pitched voice, well beyond her vocal range.

She came to the phrase: "He is the fairest of ten thousand," and her voice broke as she came to the word "ten."

Undaunted, she tried again, but met with no greater success the second time.

"Give me my note again," she requested of the pianist, and made a frantic third attempt.

"Lady," someone in the congregation called, "I don't think you're gonna make it. Don't you think you'd better start over again and try for five thousand this time?"

Kidding the Congregation

A man was going to attend a Halloween party dressed in the costume of the devil. On his way it began to rain, so he darted into a church where a revival meeting was in progress.

At the sight of his devil's costume, people began to scatter through the doors and windows.

One lady got her coat sleeve caught on the arm of one of the seats and as the man came closer she pleaded, "Satan, I've been a member of this church for twenty years, but I've really been on your side all the time."

✦

Three boys were talking and one said, "My daddy owns the laundry and three men come by every day and take the money, it's so much."

The other boy said, "My daddy owns the bank and he has a key to it."

"That's nothing," the other said, "my daddy owns hell."

"And how is that?" the other boys asked.

"Well, he came home from the deacons' meeting the other night and told Mama that they gave it to him," the boy said.

Funny Stuff

The finance committee of a church was contacting a wealthy member, who was very tight with his money. They told him that their investigation showed that he was in the high tax bracket and that they felt he should give money to the church.

The skinflint said, "Did your investigation show that I have a mother who's penniless, a sister who supports three small children since her husband was killed in an automobile wreck, and a brother who lost a leg in the war and can't support his family?"

"No," the finance committee responded.

"Well," he continued, "if I don't give to them, why should I give to the church?"

Kidding
the
Kindred

Kidding the Kindred

The parents took their little girl to an art museum to teach her how to appreciate art.

They observed a painting of the Romans throwing the Christians to the lions.

The parents realized the little girl was crying, and were gratified that she was so sympathetic. That is until she informed them why she was crying: "One of the lions didn't have a Christian to eat."

✦

A father was telling his sons for the fiftieth time his most glorious World War II adventure. "There we were," he fictionalized, "trapped, cornered like rats in an ambush, surrounded by eighty enemy soldiers. . ."

"But Dad," interrupted the smallest of his three children, "last year you said you were surrounded by only fifty enemy soldiers."

"Last year," the father continued, "you were too young to be told the whole truth."

✦

During a hurricane, a woman shook her husband and said, "Wake up, Sam. The house is shaking so much I'm sure it's going to blow away."

"Let it blow," said the husband, rolling over. "We're only renting!"

A mother whose son had been arrested by the police was called to court. An educated and progressive woman, she tried to explain her son's wayward behavior to the judge.

"Your honor," she began, "my son is one of society's angry young men. You must understand that. He's protesting against a culture that won't let him do what he wants to do."

"And what's that?" asked the judge.

"Nothing," replied the mother.

◆

"I've just been to my husband's cremation," said the widow.

"Oh, you poor thing," cried the single lady sitting by her on the plane. "I'm so sorry for you."

"He was my fourth husband," confided the widow. "I've cremated them all."

At this the stranger burst into tears.

"Have I said something to upset you?" asked the widow anxiously.

"Oh, no," she answered, still sobbing, "but I was thinking how unjust the world is! I've never had one husband and you've had husbands to burn."

Kidding the Kindred

A father promised his son a car if he would do three things: make straight A's in school, read the Bible every day, and cut his long hair.

Later, the father was checking up with his son. He said, "Son, you have made straight A's in school. You have read the Bible every day. But son, you haven't cut your hair. Why not?"

"Oh, well, Dad, Moses, Paul, and Peter all had long hair," the son remarked.

"Yes," replied the father, "but they all walked everywhere they went."

✦

A teenager was enthusiastically describing her new boyfriend to her father.

"He sounds very nice, dear," said the father, "but does he have any money?"

"Oh, you men are all alike," answered the girl. "Bob asked the same thing about you."

✦

A new bride said to her new husband at the first meal she cooked, "Dear, my mother taught me to cook and I can cook two things well: lemon pie and beef stew."

The husband, biting into the stew, said, "Fine, dear, and which is this?"

A little boy said to his mother and father, "I want a little baby sister. All my friends have baby sisters."

"Well, you pray for one, and if it's God's will, he will give you one."

He prayed for months and finally forgot it.

Then one day they took him to grandmother's, and when he returned, his father took him to his mother's bed.

His father pulled down the cover and said, "Look son, a little baby sister."

Then he pulled the cover down a little more, and another little sister.

Then he pulled the cover down a little more, and another little sister.

"Son," he said, "Aren't you glad you have three baby sisters? Aren't you glad you prayed for a baby sister?"

"Yep," the little boy replied, "but aren't you glad I quit when I did?"

◆

A widow wrote the following testimonial for a life insurance company: "On September 8, my husband took out a policy. In less than a month, he drowned. I consider insurance a good investment."

Kidding the Kindred

A West Virginia farm family had no electricity in their mountain home.

The farmer's wife was ready to deliver her first baby, so the farmer ran down the mountain and brought the doctor.

It was night, so the doctor asked the farmer to bring some light, which was a kerosene lamp.

The doctor delivered a beautiful little boy, and the farmer took the lamp back to the table.

Suddenly the doctor said, "Bring the light back," and the doctor delivered a beautiful little girl. He took the lamp back to the table.

The doctor said, "Hurry, bring the light back."

The farmer said, "Doc, you don't think they're attracted to the light, do you?"

An old mountaineer and his son went to the city for the first time. In a modern building, he saw an elevator open, an old woman step in, and the doors close.

Soon another elevator opened its doors and a young woman stepped out.

The old mountaineer said, "Son, you stay right here. I'm going for your mother to run her through that machine."

A person called his friend and a small voice said, "Hello?"

"May I speak to your mother?"

"No, she is busy."

"Is there anybody else there?"

"Yes, a policeman."

"May I speak to him?"

"No, he's busy."

"Is there anybody else there?"

"Yes, a fireman."

"May I speak to him?"

"No, he's busy."

"Your mother, a policeman, and a fireman all are busy. What are they doing?"

"Looking for me."

✦

There was the little boy who approached Santa in a department store with a long list of requests. He wanted a bicycle and a sled, a chemistry set, a cowboy suit, a train set, a baseball glove, and roller skates.

"That's a pretty long list," Santa said sternly. "I'll have to check in my book and see if you were a good boy."

"No, no." the youngster said quickly. "Never mind checking. I'll just take the roller skates."

Kidding the Kindred

A husband raced into the house and said to his wife, "I've found a great job. The salary is good. It offers free medical insurance and paid holidays."

"That's wonderful, dear," his wife said.

"I thought you'd be pleased," the husband said. "You start tomorrow."

✦

The husband died and the wife didn't know how much money he had left her. She knew he had a lot saved, but she had never known the amount.

She didn't have much money of her own, but she spent most of it on a very beautiful tombstone for him with the words "Rest In Peace" engraved on it.

Later they read the husband's will and she found he had left her very little, but left most of it to his secretary.

The wife was furious, and called the tombstone company and asked them to change the inscription. They said it would cost a lot of money since they would have to make a complete new one.

"But," the salesman added, "we could add some words to the existing words."

"That's fine," the widow said. "To the words 'Rest In Peace' add 'Until I Come.' "

Funny Stuff

Junior: "Dad, what makes an elephant so big?"

Father: "I don't know."

Junior: "Why is a lion dangerous?"

Father: "I don't know, son."

Junior: "Am I bothering you with my questions, Dad?"

Father: "Not at all. You never learn anything if you don't ask."

◆

A man in jail wrote his wife, "Don't plant the potatoes—that's where I buried the money."

She wrote her husband, "The sheriff censored your letter and they have dug up the whole backyard."

The husband wrote back, "Now is the time to plant the potatoes."

◆

A wife told her husband, "You never tell me you love me."

"Oh, yes, I did," he replied. "I told you that when we were married."

"But that was twenty years ago," she sighed.

"Okay," he answered, "I love you. This time, don't forget it."

Kidding the Kindred

A woman entered a plane with a newborn infant in her arms. A drunk man sat down next to her. He took one look at the baby and said, "Ma'am, I've never seen anything more repulsive in my life. Your baby is the ugliest thing I've ever set my eyes on."

Diplomatically the stewardess led the drunk man to another seat in the rear of the plane. Then she rushed back to the lady passenger. "I'm terribly sorry this had to happen," she explained. "Now you just relax—I'll bring you a hot cup of coffee and I'll dig up a banana for your little monkey."

◆

A little boy was making quite a mess at the table. His father scolded him, "Son, you eat like a pig."

Realizing his little boy had never seen a pig, he said, "You do know what a pig is, don't you, son?"

"Yes," he replied. "It's a hog's little boy."

◆

A father was buying a fountain pen for his son's birthday gift. "I suppose it's to be a surprise, sir," said the clerk.

"I'll say it is," replied the father. "He's expecting a new car!"

A man, seventy-eight, in perfect health, decided to join a retirement center. The first day he noticed a lady watching his every move. Everywhere he went she stared.

The second day it was the same. The third day, the same.

He just couldn't take any more. So, he said, "Madam, why do you stare at me all of the time?"

"Sir," she said, "you look exactly like my fourth husband."

"How many times have you been married?" he asked.

She replied, "Three."

◆

The young son of a well-known television star came home from school with his report card.

"Well, Son," said the father, "were you promoted?"

"Better than that, Dad," replied the youngster. "I was held over for another twenty-six weeks."

◆

A Sunday school teacher was describing how Lot's wife looked back and turned to a pillar of salt.

Little Jack interrupted, "My mother looked back and turned into a telephone pole."

Kidding the Kindred

Mother: "Son, didn't I hear the clock strike two as you came home last night?"

Teenaged son: "You did, Mom. It started to strike ten, but I stopped it to keep it from waking you up!"

◆

An eight-year-old boy had been pestering his father for a watch. Finally his father said in exasperation, "I don't want to hear about your wanting a watch again."

At dinner that night the family each gave a Scripture verse at the dinner table, and the boy repeated Mark 13:37. "And what I say unto you I say unto all, Watch."

◆

The lawyer gathered the family of the recently deceased Sam Berg around him.

He began to read Sam's will aloud: "To my dear wife, I leave my house, fifty acres of land, and one million dollars. To my son, Sam, I leave my two cars and $100,000. To my daughter, Bessie, I leave my yacht and $100,000. And to my brother-in-law, who always insisted that health is better than wealth, I leave my sun lamp."

Funny Stuff

The teenage daughter had been on the family telephone for half an hour. When finally she did hang up, her father said sarcastically, "You usually talk for two hours. What stopped you this time?"

"Wrong number," replied his daughter.

✦

Said one father to another: "Of course two people can live as cheaply as one. My wife and I live as cheaply as our daughter in college!"

✦

The young bee-bop enthusiast bought every record that made the top ten in the jazz world. One day she phoned her local music store, but accidentally dialed the wrong number and got the plumbing company by mistake.

The conversation went something like this: "Hello, do you have 'Ten Little Fingers and Ten Little Toes in Alabama?' "

A deep bass voice on the other end of the line replied, "No, ma'am, but I have a wife and thirteen kids in Texas."

"Is that a record?" the young lady asked.

"No, ma'am," the deep voice replied, "but I'm sure it's much above the average."

Kidding the Kindred

A lady had been married four times. Her first husband was a banker, the second an actor, the third a minister, and the fourth an undertaker. When asked why the different ones she said: "One for the money, two for the show, three to get ready, and four to go."

✦

"Horrors, Bobby!" mother exclaimed. "Just look at you! Face dirty and scratched, clothes muddy, one shoe off. How many times have I told you never to play with that bad Smith boy?"

Bobby looked up at her, aggrieved. "Do I look like I've been playing?"

✦

A little boy was saying his go-to-bed prayers in a very low voice.

"I can't hear you, dear," his mother whispered.

"Wasn't talking to you," said the boy firmly.

✦

A little boy getting ready for bed interrupted a family gathering in the living room to say, "I'm going up to say my prayers now. Anybody want anything?"

"Do you," the judge asked the groom, "take this woman for better or for worse, through sickness and health, in good times and in bad, whether she be. . ."

"Confound it, judge," broke in the bride, "you're gonna talk him right out of it!"

◆

A man was taking a census in a rural mountain neighborhood.

A little boy came to the door and the man asked, "May I see your mother?"

"Oh, she's in the asylum."

"Well, may I see your father?"

"Oh, he's in jail."

"Well, how about a brother or sister?"

"I have a sister in the reform school. . .and, oh, yes, I have a brother at Harvard."

"That's strange. What's he studying?"

"Oh, he ain't studying nothing, mister. They're studying him."

◆

My son has everything in his room—a record player, TV, VCR, you name it.

So, when I punish him, I have to make him go to my room.

Kidding the Kindred

"Darling," I said to my wife, "I have tickets for the theater."

She said, "Oh, that's wonderful. I'll start dressing at once."

I said, "Yes, please do, honey, the tickets are for tomorrow night."

✦

They were arguing violently over her selection of a fiancé.

"But mother," she cried, "he said he'd put the earth at my feet."

"My darling," mother said, calming down, "you already have the earth at your feet. What you'll be needing is a roof over your head."

✦

A boy received an FBI set for Christmas.

His dad said, "Son, did you know that all fingerprints are different? No two are the same."

The son said, "No, Dad, I know three people who have the same fingerprints."

"Well now, who are these three people who have the same fingerprints?"

The son said, "One is my dad, another is Santa Claus, and the other is that rascal who steals money from Mom's cookie jar."

On the first night of his grandmother's visit, a small boy was saying his prayers.

"Please, God," he shouted, "send me a bicycle, a tool chest, a. . ."

"Why are you praying so loud?" his older brother interrupted. "God isn't deaf."

"I know He isn't," replied the boy. "But Grandma is."

A teacher was examining her fifth graders on what they remembered about the various words that Jesus spoke. One of her questions was this: "What did Jesus say about people getting married?"

Little Johnny blurted out: "Jesus said: 'Father, forgive them, for they know not what they do.' "

A student went to the college psychiatrist and said, "I'll never be able to trust my parents again after the low, deceitful, sneaky thing they just did to me."

The psychiatrist asked, "What did they do?"

The kid said, "I asked them to send me $600 for a set of encyclopedias—and they sent me the encyclopedias!"

Kidding the Kindred

Teacher (answering the telephone): "You say
    Tommy Smith has a bad cold and can't come
    to school? Who is this speaking?"
Hoarse voice: "This is my father."

A poor widow's son down in Texas struck it rich
with oil and, as Mother's Day approached, made
up his mind to show his appreciation by some
unusual gift for all his mother had done for him.
So he told the owner of a pet shop that he wanted
the most unusual and expensive pet he had.

The merchant replied, "I have a myna bird
worth $27,000. It is the only one in the world that
can recite the Lord's Prayer, the 23rd Psalm and
the 13th chapter of First Corinthians.

"I'll take it," said the Texan. "I don't care how
much it costs. Mom is worth it and she will get so
much comfort hearing it recite Scripture."

So he bought it and shipped it off to his mother.

On Monday following Mother's Day, he called
her long distance. "Did you get my bird?" he
asked.

"Yes, Son."

"How did you like it?"

"It was delicious, Son."

A lady wrote to the advice column in a newspaper: "I have been engaged to a man for some time, but just before the wedding, I find he has a wooden leg. Do you think I should break it off?"

✦

Little Willie asked, "Mother, what becomes of an automobile when it gets too old to run?"

She answered, "Some smart salesman pawns it off on your father."

✦

"What pretty hair you have, Mary," said the visitor. "You must have gotten it from your mother."

"No," replied little Mary. "I must have gotten it from Daddy. His is all gone!"

✦

A young daughter watched her mother apply cream to her face. "What's that for, Mother?"

"That's to make me beautiful," the Mother replied.

A half hour later the daughter watched as the cream was being removed.

She studied seriously for a minute and said, "Didn't work, did it, Mother?"

Esmerelda had been listening intently to her husband Bertram. He was pleased. "I'm happy to see you're impressed by my lecture on economics and banking," said he.

"Yes," she nodded. "I'm enthralled at the fact that anybody can know so much about money without having any."

✦

Bride's father to groom: "My boy, you're the second happiest man in the world!"

✦

Lou: "My wife had a dream last night that she was married to a millionaire."

Bob: "You're lucky. My wife thinks that in the daytime."

✦

Last month my wife decided to save money on electricity. We didn't turn on any lights; we didn't watch TV; we didn't play the radio; we even unplugged the refrigerator. The electric bill for thirty-one days was eight cents. It would have been zero but the electric company kept ringing the bell to find out what was wrong!

Robert Long and his sixteen-year-old son share the same first names.

One evening the telephone rang and a youngster asked to speak to Bob.

"Do you mean Senior or Junior?" asked Mr. Long.

"Neither," the caller replied. "The one I want is a sophomore."

✦

A proud father brought home a backyard swing set for his kids. Immediately, he started to assemble it, with all the neighborhood kids waiting to swing.

After several hours of attempting to put bolt A into slot B, he gave up. Finally, he saw the old handyman working in a neighbor's yard and asked him to help him.

The old-timer came over and immediately threw the directions away and in a short time had the set assembled.

"It's beyond me, friend," he said. "How did you assemble this set without reading the directions?"

"To tell you the truth," the handyman said, "When you can't read, you've got to think."

Kidding the Kindred

Two fathers were discussing the return to college of their respective sons:

"What's your boy studying to be?" asked the one.

"From his letters," said the father, "we think he'll be a professional fund-raiser."

◆

A little boy asked his father, "How was I born?"

He said, "The stork brought you."

"Well, how were you born?"

"The stork brought me," the father replied.

Later he asked his grandfather how he was born, and the grandfather said, "The stork brought me."

The boy was to write a paper at school about birth, and he wrote, "We haven't had a natural birth in our family in three generations."

◆

A lady at the Super Bowl was asked why the seat next to her was empty.

"It was my husband's seat, but he died."

"I'm surprised that some of his relatives didn't use it."

"Oh," she replied, "they're all attending the funeral."

A father was examining his son's report card. "One thing is definitely in your favor," he announced. "With this report card, you couldn't possibly be cheating."

✦

Hubby: "I can't eat this cake!"
Wife: "Well, I followed the instructions of this recipe which I clipped from a magazine."
Hubby: "Then you must have used the other side of the clipping: 'How to Make a Rock Garden.' "

✦

After a day of complete harassment, the mother shook her finger at her small, unruly youngster and shouted, "All right, junior. Do anything you please! Now, let me see you disobey that!"

✦

A mother corrected her son when he said he was sweating.

She said a person perspires and a horse sweats.

One day it was very hot and he said, "I am perspiring so much. I'm sweating like a horse."

Kidding the Kindred

The son asked his mother a question, and she said, "Go ask your daddy."

The boy replied, "I don't think I want to know that much about it."

✦

A boy said to his father, "Dad, the principal said for me to invite you to a small meeting at the school."

"How small is it, Son?" the father asked.

"It's you and me and the principal," he replied.

✦

"Yes," said the old man to his visitor, "I am proud of my girls and I would like to see them comfortably married. As I have made a little money, they will not go penniless to their husbands. There is Mary, twenty-five years old, and a good-looking girl. I'll give her $1,000 when she marries.

"Then comes Elizabeth, who won't see thirty-five again. I shall give her $3,000, and the man who takes Eliza, who is forty, will have $5,000 with her."

The visitor, an enterprising young man, reflected a moment and asked: "You haven't a daughter about fifty, have you, sir?"

Funny Stuff

The young couples' Sunday school class was studying the story of Abraham and Sarah, who in their nineties were blessed with a child. Among other things the teacher asked, "What lesson do we learn from this story?"

A young mother of three who was having financial difficulties blurted out: "They waited until they could afford it!"

✦

Here's a suggestion for parents who become naturally worried when their youngsters are away from home, either at camp or college, and neglect to write:

Send the child your usual letter and add this postscript: "Hope you can use the $50.00 I am enclosing."

✦

One six-year-old cutie-pie had been naughty and was duly scolded by both parents. At supper, immediately after the hassle, a contrite Papa and Mama asked little Betsy if she would like to say grace. She bowed her sweet curly head and murmured, "I thank Thee, Lord, that Thou hast prepared a table for me in the presence of mine enemies."

Kidding the Kindred

The small boy was quizzing his father. He asked, "Is it true that the stork brings babies?"

"Yes, Sonny."

"And Christmas presents come from Santa Claus?"

"Yes, Sonny."

"And the Lord gives us our daily bread?"

"Yes, Sonny."

"Then daddy, why do we need you?"

The five-year-old boy was busily drawing and his mother inquired what it was.

"I'm drawing a picture of Adam and Eve," said the boy.

"But nobody knows what Adam and Eve looked like," said the mother.

"They will," replied the boy, "when I get through."

A newlywed was asked how she liked married life.

She replied, "Oh, I hate it."

"Why?"

"You make those dirty old beds, wash those dirty old dishes, and wash those dirty old clothes. And in two weeks, you do it all over again."

A young lad with very long hair walked into a barber shop, sat down and began looking through the magazines. Eventually, the barber beckoned to him, "Next!"

"Oh, I don't want anything," the boy said.

"No haircut?" replied the barber. "Then why did you come in?"

"My mother is looking for me," the long-haired lad answered, "and I don't think she'll look in here."

✦

A little boy just couldn't learn. One day his teacher asked him who signed the Declaration of Independence. He didn't know. For almost a week she asked him the same question every day, but still he couldn't come up with the right answer.

Finally, in desperation, she called the boy's father to her office. "Your boy won't tell me who signed the Declaration of Independence," she complained.

"Come here, Son, and sit down," the dad said to the boy. "Now if you signed the crazy thing, admit it, and let's get out of here."

Kidding the Kindred

A father and son wanted to hunt on a friend's property, so they called him and made arrangements for a date.

Early in the morning they arrived on the appointed day, and the son went up to the friend's house and told him that they were ready to start the hunt.

The friend told the son where to hunt and asked him to do him a little favor. "When you pass the barn shoot that old mule. He's about forty years old, but we don't have the heart to kill him."

The son, thinking he could have a little fun with his father, said, "Dad, that so-and-so friend of ours wouldn't let us hunt on his property so I think I'll just walk over there and kill his mule."

He grabbed his gun, walked over and shot the old mule.

He started back to the car when he heard *bang, bang* and his father yelling, "You were right about our friend, Son, so I killed two cows."

Kidding the Kids

Kidding the Kids

A Sunday school teacher was reviewing with her fifth graders the events in the life of Jesus that impressed them the most and the happenings they liked best. These were some of the responses: When Jesus raised Lazarus from the dead; when He raised the twelve-year-old girl to life; when He helped the apostles catch so many fish their boat began to sink. But little Eddie took the prize when he declared: "I like the story about the big crowd that loafs and fishes."

◆

Eight-year-old Billy had a crush on seven-year-old Betty. For Valentine's Day he sent her a small but pretty box of chocolates. With it was this tender note: "To Betty, with all my allowance—Billy."

◆

A minister was preaching and said: "Who wants to go to heaven?"

Everybody held up his hand except one young boy.

"Son, don't you want to go to heaven when you die?"

"Yes, sir, when I die, but I thought you was getting up a load to go now."

Funny Stuff

A youngster stood gazing intently at his father's visitor, a homely man of large proportions. At length the man became a bit embarrassed and said, "Well, my boy, what are you looking at me for?"

"Why," replied the boy, "Daddy told Mother that you were a self-made man and I want to see what you look like."

"Quite right," said the gratified guest. "I am a self-made man."

The boy asked with considerable surprise, "But why did you make yourself like that?"

The late G. Campbell Morgan related this story of his granddaughter, Penelope, a precocious child, who later became a radiant Christian worker and witness.

One day Penelope rushed indoors shouting, "Oh, Mother, there's a big black bear in the backyard!"

"You know perfectly well it's only a big dog," said her mother. "Now go to your room and ask God to forgive you for telling a lie."

"Did you ask God to forgive you?" she asked when Penelope came downstairs a little later.

"Yes," Penelope replied, "and He said it was quite all right. He thought it was a bear Himself when He first saw it."

Kidding the Kids

A schoolteacher was quizzing her pupils about honesty in all things. "Suppose," she asked the class, "you were walking along Main Street, and you found a briefcase that contained $500,000 in cash. What would you do?"

In the back row little Johnny raised both his hands. The teacher called on him.

"Well," said Johnny, "if it belonged to a poor family, I'd return it."

◆

Two boys were playing marbles together when a very pretty little girl walked by.

One boy stopped and said to his pal, "Boy, when I stop hating girls, she's the one I'm going to stop hating first."

◆

A little boy was selling postcards for ten cents.

A man said, "Son, what are you going to do with the money?"

"I'm raising a million dollars to feed all the starving people all over the world," he replied.

"Do you expect to raise it all by yourself?" he asked.

"No, sir," replied the little boy. "There's another little boy helping me."

A father was teaching his son to admire the beauties of nature.

"Look, son," he exclaimed, "isn't that a beautiful picture God has painted?"

"It sure is, Dad," responded the youngster enthusiastically, "especially since God had to paint it with His left hand."

The father was baffled, "What do you mean, son, His left hand?"

"Well," answered the boy, "my Sunday school teacher said that Jesus was sitting on God's right hand."

✦

Little Mary, just home from her first day of school, was asked by her mother, "Well, darling, what did you learn today?"

"Not much," replied Mary. "I've got to go back tomorrow."

✦

The Sunday school teacher, trying to get some response from his class of eight-year-old boys, said, "Boys, don't you imagine old Noah, on that ark, spent a lot of time fishing?"

A bright kid piped up, "I don't imagine he did. He didn't have but two worms."

A boy used bad grammar in school. He always said, "I have 'rote' my lesson."

His teacher said, "It is 'written,' not 'rote,' and I want you to write on the blackboard 'it is written' 100 times."

When she came back into the classroom she found a note that said, "I have rote 'it is written' 100 times, and now I have went home."

At the weekly Scout meeting the Scoutmaster asked each boy who had done his good deed for the day to raise his hand. All hands shot up, with the exception of one little boy.

"Now you go out," ordered the Scoutmaster, "and don't come back until you have done a good deed."

About twenty minutes later the lad returned in a disheveled condition, with his shirt badly torn.

"Well, did you do your good deed for today?" inquired the Scoutmaster.

"Yes," replied the boy.

"What is it?" asked the Scoutmaster.

"I helped an old lady across the street."

"And how did you get in such a mess?"

"She didn't want to go," meekly mused the boy.

Funny Stuff

A Sunday school class was ready for its question and answer session.

"What is it that we learn from the story of Jonah and the whale?" the teacher asked.

A bright kid spoke up and said, "What we learned is that people make whales sick."

A young son was bad about telling lies.

One day his father decided to tell his son such a big lie that the boy would be cured from stretching the truth.

"Son," he said, "one day I was walking down the street, and a twenty-thousand-pound gorilla grabbed me, and threw me down, and was ready to throw me over the building, when a little two-and-a-half pound dog came up and threw that gorilla up a tree, and I got away. Son, do you believe that?"

"Yes, Pop, that was my dog."

Small boy's prayer: "Dear God, take care of Mommy and Daddy and Sister and Aunt Jenny and Uncle Jim and Grandma and Grandpa, and please God, take care of Yourself, or else we're all sunk!"

Kidding the Kids

A teacher asked the kindergartners, "Can a bear take his warm overcoat off?"

"No," they answered.

"Why not?"

Finally, after a long silence, a little fellow spoke up. "Because only God knows where the buttons are."

Sunday school teacher: "Now, Charlie, what can you tell me about Goliath?"
Charlie: "Goliath was the man David rocked to sleep."

Laughing
at
Lawyers

An attorney told his client, "You pay $1000 now and $500 a month for thirty-six months."

"That sounds like buying a car," replied the client.

The lawyer nodded. "I am."

✦

A man received a large bill from his lawyer. Shortly thereafter, the man met the attorney on the street and said, "It's a beautiful day today."

Then he added, "Remember, I'm telling you, not asking."

✦

A boy and his father were walking through a cemetery reading the epitaphs. He found one tombstone that read: "Here lies a lawyer and an honest man."

"Look here, Daddy," the boy called. "They buried two men in one grave!"

✦

Judge: "Couldn't this case have been settled out of court?"

Defendant: "Yes, sir, and that's exactly what we were trying to do when the police butted in."

A Hollywood actor was testifying in an accident case, and was asked to identify himself. "I am probably the world's greatest actor," he told the court.

The next day his girlfriend chided him. "Don't you think," she said, "you laid it on a little too thick yesterday?"

"Ordinarily," said the ham, "I avoid any kind of self-praise. But, don't forget, this time I was under oath."

A young man, just graduated from law school, opened a brand new office but no clients came.

Then a man finally walked into the office. The lawyer thought he had better make a good impression, so he grabbed the phone and said, "Yes, yes, I'm so sorry I can't take your case today. I have an appointment with the officials of a large corporation. I'm so sorry."

Returning to the visitor, the attorney said, "Now, what can I do for you?"

"Oh, nothing," the man replied. "I've come from the telephone company to connect your phone."

Laughing at Lawyers

One of the greatest criminal lawyers in the nation got an urgent phone call from one of his clients.

The caller said, "I'm in prison and they've shaved my head, transferred me to death row, and cut a slit in my trousers. What should I do?"

Replied the lawyer, "Don't sit down."

Laughing
with
Legislators

"Dad, what's a traitor in politics?"

"Well, Son, a traitor is a man who deserts our party and goes over to the opposition."

"I see. Well, what's a man who leaves the other party and comes across to ours?"

"That's different, Son. He's a convert."

◆

How do you know when a politician is telling the truth?

When he pulls his ear, he is telling the truth; when he rubs his nose, he is telling the truth; but when he opens his mouth, he is lying.

◆

When Columbus started out, he didn't know where he was going. When he got there, he didn't know where he was. When he got back, he didn't know where he had been. And he did all of it on other people's money.

What a politician Columbus would have been.

◆

You have got to give George Washington credit. There he was surrounded by trouble and he couldn't blame the previous administration.

Funny Stuff

Soon after he had been elected governor of New York State, Al Smith visited Sing Sing Prison. He was asked to have lunch and after lunch to say a few words to the prisoners.

He cleared his throat and began, "Fellow Democrats," but he quickly caught himself, knowing no good Democrat should be in prison.

He started again: "Fellow citizens," but caught himself suddenly again, knowing that criminals often lost their citizenship.

So he backed up and said, "My friends, I'm glad to see you all here."

◆

A well-known politician asked one of the opposition to lend him a quarter. "I want to call one of my friends," he explained.

"Here's fifty cents," offered the other. "Call all of your friends."

◆

A sidewalk interviewer asked a retired man what he thought of the two candidates for an election.

"When I look at them," the retired man replied, "I'm thankful only one of them can get elected."

Kelly and Murphy were next-door neighbors. One evening, over the backyard fence, they were discussing the candidates in the coming election.

Said Kelly: "I feel that I shouldn't vote for any of the candidates. I don't know any of them."

To which Murphy added: "I don't know how to vote either. I know all of them."

Lyndon B. Johnson used cue cards when he made a speech.

Just before one of his important speeches, Johnson fired his cue card maker after the man had made the cards for an important speech.

During the speech Johnson read from cue card number one: "They say we can't protect our country without additional taxes, but I say we can."

Then he read cue card number two. "They say we cannot have prosperity in our nation without higher taxes, but I say we can."

Then he turned to cue card number three and read, "Okay, Lyndon, you are on your own."

"Well," the little old lady finally admitted to the persistent politician, "you're my second choice."

"I'm honored, ma'am," he gushed. "But may I ask—who's your first?"

"Oh," she responded casually, "anybody else who's running."

Marital Mirth

A preacher went to the mountains to preach. Upon arriving, he struck up a conversation with the first man he met.

"Are you a Christian?" the preacher inquired.

"Nope, Mr. Christian lives up the holler," answered the mountaineer.

"What I mean is: Brother, are you lost?" persisted the preacher.

"Well, I reckon not," replied the mountaineer. "I have been here nigh on to thirty years and know every cow path in these here hills."

"You don't understand," said the preacher. "I mean, are you ready for the Judgment Day?"

"When's it comin'?" asked the mountaineer.

"Well," said the preacher, "it might come today or it might be tomorrow."

"For goodness sakes, don't tell my missus," cautioned the man. "She'd want to go both days!"

◆

A grouchy husband came down to breakfast one morning. His wife had prepared orange juice and two eggs—one fried, one scrambled. He very sourly said, "Yep, just as I thought, you've done it again."

"Now what's wrong?" she asked.

"As usual, you fried the wrong egg," he shouted.

A man-about-town was sitting in the barber's chair having a shave and manicure.

"You're cute," he said to the pretty young manicurist. "How about a date tonight?"

The manicurist smiled and said, "I'm sorry, but you see, I'm married."

"Big deal," said the man-about-town. "Phone the bum and tell him you'll be home late tonight."

"You tell him," said the manicurist sweetly. "He's shaving you."

✦

The wife turned to her husband and asked, "Will you love me when my hair turns gray?"

"Why not?" he said. "Haven't I loved you through five other shades?"

✦

Right in the middle of the service, and just before the sermon, one of the congregation remembered she had forgotten to turn off the gas under the roast. Hurriedly, she scribbled a note and passed it to the usher to give to her husband.

Unfortunately, the usher misunderstood her intention and took it to the pulpit. Unfolding the note, the preacher read aloud: "Please go home and turn off the gas."

An evangelist took his young son shopping in a grocery store. He was in the shopping cart. At the first aisle he saw some chocolate cookies. He said, "I want just four of those chocolate cookies."

"No son, we're in a hurry," said his father.

The next aisle, he remembered the chocolate cookies, and whimpered, "I want just three of those chocolate cookies."

"No, we're in a big hurry," said his father.

The next aisle, he thought of the cookies again, and said pleadingly, "Please get me just two chocolate cookies."

"No," said the father, "we're in a big hurry."

Then when they got to the checkout counter, the little boy stood up in the shopping cart, threw up his hands and cried at the top of his voice, "In the name of Jesus, give me just one chocolate cookie."

A young man was proposing to his girlfriend:

"Honey, I love you, but I wish I could give you the things my friend Benny has—boats, cars, airplanes—but honey, I really love you."

She replied, "I love you too, baby, but tell me more about Benny."

The man and his wife arrived at the boarding gate in time to see their plane taking off. He was extremely upset about having missed the plane.

"If you weren't so slow in getting ready we wouldn't have missed the plane," he complained.

"And if you hadn't rushed me so, we wouldn't have so long to wait for the next flight," she replied.

✦

Dave told his wife Marylou he would take her out to dine royally.

Later Marylou reported, "We started out at Burger King and wound up at the Dairy Queen."

✦

The English professor at school, over and over again, emphasized the importance of developing an extensive vocabulary.

"You have my assurance," he told the class, "that if you repeat a word eight or ten times, it will be yours for life."

In the rear row, an attractive young woman sighed and, closing her blue eyes, muttered softly to herself, "Steve, Steve, Steve."

A woman on a television audience-participation show was asked the name of her favorite author.

"Why, it's my husband," she replied.

"Your husband?" questioned the interviewer. "What does he write?"

The woman smiled brightly, then answered: "Checks."

✦

The officious neighbor lady disapproved of Mr. McTavish and his autocratic methods. "If I were your wife," said the busybody, a gal devoid of personal charm, "I'd give you poison."

Mr. McTavish bowed courteously and said, "And madam, if I were your husband, I'd take it."

✦

The television polltaker asked: "Do you have your television set on, sir?"

"Yes," replied the man.

"Are other members of your family with you?" the pollster continued.

"Yes, my wife is here."

"To whom are you listening, sir?"

"My wife."

An ardent golfer was on the putting green, when suddenly a woman came running up the fairway with her wedding gown flying.

"How could you do this to me?"

"Listen," he said, "I told you, only if it rained."

◆

"My husband didn't leave a bit of insurance."

"Then where did you get that gorgeous diamond ring?"

"Well, he left a thousand dollars for a casket and five thousand dollars for a stone. This is the stone."

"Darling," she cooed, "would you like some tender chops, nice browned potatoes, string beans, and a delicious apple pie with cheese?"

"No," he answered wearily. "Let's eat at home and save money."

◆

A man was walking with his wife and they stopped at the scales in front of a drugstore.

"Are you overweight, dear?" he asked.

"No," she gasped, "but according to this chart, I should be six inches taller."

A man wasn't feeling very good, so he went to his doctor for an examination. The doctor said, "Come back in a couple of weeks and I'll give you the results of the test."

When the man returned, the doctor said, "I have some bad news for you. You only have a short time to live. About nine months."

The man was very concerned, and asked, "What you would do if you were in my place?"

The doctor thought for a minute and said, "Number one: I would move to North Dakota; number two: I'd buy a pig farm; and number three: I'd marry a widow with eight children."

He thought about that and he said, "I don't understand, Doctor. If I did that would it make me live longer?"

"No, it won't, but those will be the longest nine months of your life."

He had proposed and the girl had turned him down.

"Ah, well," he sighed dejectedly, "I suppose I'll never marry now."

The girl couldn't help laughing a little, she was so flattered.

"You silly boy!" she said. "Because I've turned you down, that doesn't mean that other girls will do the same."

"Of course it does," he returned with a faint smile. "If you won't have me, who will?"

Medical Mirth

Barney began shouting at his physician, "You're nothing but a quack. You've had me come back for unnecessary treatments for six months. You've taken my money without helping me. You've gotten rich on my case alone!"

"That's gratitude," said the doctor. "And to think I named my new yacht after you."

✦

Recently my brother was told that he'd have to undergo a kidney operation.

"Let me advise you now," said the surgeon, "of how I work. I believe in getting my patients up and around very quickly. Three hours following the operation you'll sit up. Five hours later, you'll stand up. The next day you'll be walking."

"Fine," my brother agreed. "But will you let me lie down during the operation?"

✦

After careful examination," said the doctor to his patient, "I'm sorry to tell you that you have only four hours to live. Is there anyone you would like to see before you go?"

"Yes," answered the patient. "Another doctor."

After the doctor checked the patient over, he asked, "Have you been living a normal life?"

"Yes, doctor," replied the patient.

"Well, you'll have to cut it out for awhile."

◆

Doctor to portly patient: "Follow this diet, and in a couple of months, I want to see three-fourths of you back here for a checkup."

◆

A doctor asked his new patient if she had been to any other doctor about her complaint, before coming to see him.

"No," she replied, and then added, "but I did go to see my druggist."

"Well, that shows just how much sense some people have!" he exclaimed. "And what sort of silly advice did your druggist give you?"

"Oh," she answered sweetly, "he told me to see you."

◆

When they wheeled a man into the operating room and raised his gown, the surgeon found a piece of tape pasted across his abdomen, which read, "Think."

The phone rang at 4 A.M. and the doctor picked it up. A woman asked, "How much do you charge for a house call?"

"Ten dollars," the physician answered sleepily.

"How much for an office visit?"

"Five," the doctor replied.

"Okay," snapped the woman. "I'll meet you in your office in half an hour."

✦

The lady visited the doctor's office every week with a new complaint, although, in fact, she was in fine health. This week her ailment was that she was growing hard of hearing.

"It's so bad," she said, "I can't hear myself cough."

The doctor nodded patiently and filled out a prescription.

"Will this improve my hearing?" the lady asked.

"No," replied the doctor, "but it will help you to cough louder."

✦

I just got a physical and asked the doctor, "Doc, how do I stand?"

He said, "That's what puzzles me."

Patient: "Nurse, I've got a bad case of arthritis,
    there's a painful buzzing in my ears, I have a
    sprained ankle, my thumb is out of joint; and I
    see spots before my eyes."

Nurse: "But you must be awfully healthy to stand
    all that pain."

✦

Patient to doctor after operation: "Why are all the
    shades down?"

Doctor: "There's a fire across the street and I
    didn't want you to wake up thinking the
    operation was a failure."

✦

An elderly man visited a doctor for a thorough
physical examination. Upon finishing the examination the doctor said, "You're as fit as a fiddle.
You'll live to be eighty."

    "But, I am eighty!" the patient exclaimed.

    The doctor smiled. "See, what did I tell you?"

✦

Mother: "Now, Junior, be a good boy and say
    'Ahhh' so the doctor can get his finger out of
    your mouth."

A quack doctor was bragging about his famous herb tonic to a rural audience.

"Yes, gentlemen," he said, "I have sold this tonic for over twenty-five years and never heard a word of complaint. Now what does that prove?"

A voice in the crowd replied: "That dead men don't tell lies."

✦

"I'm Dr. Hamilton's nurse," a sweet voice announced to a well-known Hollywood writer, "and the reason I'm phoning you, sir, is to tell you that your check came back."

"Just tell the doctor," the writer answered, "so did my arthritis."

✦

George was having trouble with a toothache, so he decided to visit the dentist.

"What do you charge for extracting a tooth?" George asked.

"Five dollars," replied the dentist.

"Five dollars for only two seconds of work?" exclaimed George.

"Well," replied the dentist, "if you wish, I can extract it more slowly."

A fellow was playing golf and met his doctor coming off the course. He said to his doctor, "How did you do today?"

The doctor said, "I broke 100."

The man said, "Strokes?"

The physician replied, "No, appointments."

◆

A man went on a diet recommended by his doctor.

He returned in a week and said he hadn't lost a pound. The doctor said, "Stay on your diet."

The man returned in two weeks and said, "I not only did not lose, but I gained five pounds."

The doctor said, "Are you sure you have not been eating anything else except your diet food?"

"Nothing, doctor, except my regular meals."

◆

A doctor, who was superintendent of the Sunday school in a small village, asked one of the boys this question: "Willie, will you tell me what we must do in order to get to heaven?"

Said Willie, "We must die."

"Very true," replied the doctor, "but tell me what we must do before we die."

"We must get sick," said Willie, "and send for you."

A man visited his doctor for a checkup. He made some tests and called him the next week.

The doctor said, "Friend, I have some good and some bad news for you. Which do you want first?"

"The good," the patient said.

"The good news is, you only have two days to live," the doctor said.

"Man, what could be worse? What is the bad news?"

"I forgot to call you yesterday."

A hypochondriac told his doctor in great alarm that he was sure he had a fatal liver disease.

"Nonsense!" protested the doctor. "You would never know if you had the disease or not. With that ailment there is no discomfort of any kind."

"I know," gasped the patient. "My symptoms exactly."

A dentist is examining a patient. "My, that's a large cavity. My, that's a large cavity."

The patient sits up indignantly and exclaims, "I know that and you didn't have to repeat it!"

The dentist responds: "I didn't repeat it. That was the echo."

A rich man had been visiting his psychiatrist every day for several months. He lay on the couch and went to sleep every time. After he awoke he paid a $25 fee for the visit.

The doctor was disturbed that the man never talked, and one day said, "Now I want you to think of something and ask me about it."

After a few minutes of silence, the old man suddenly bolted upright from the couch. The doctor said, "Do you have something to ask?"

"Yes," replied the man. "You don't need a partner, do you?"

✦

Patient: "Doctor, what I need is something to stir me up. Something to put me in fighting trim. Did you put anything like that in this prescription?"

Doctor: "No. You'll find that in the bill."

✦

A boy telephoned the dentist's office and said, "I'm supposed to make an appointment."

"I'm sorry," replied the nurse, "but the doctor is out of town."

"Thank you," the boy responded. "When will he be out of town again?"

A man visited a doctor and said that every time he pressed his finger against any part of his body it hurt really bad. He showed the doctor by pressing his finger against his shoulder. "Oh, it really hurts," he shouted. Then he pressed his finger against his stomach. "That really hurts too," he sighed. Then he pressed his leg. "That really hurt," he moaned.

The doctor examined him thoroughly and said, "I can't find anything wrong with your shoulder, leg, or stomach, so I'm going to send you to a specialist."

He went to a specialist who examined him and said, "Friend, you have a broken finger."

✦

A psychiatrist received a postcard from one of his clients vacationing in Rome: "Having a terrific time. Wish you were here to tell me why."

✦

When the farmer was admitted into the doctor's office, he mumbled, "Shore hope I'm sick."

The doctor said, "That certainly is a poor attitude!"

"Y'see, doc," replied the farmer, "I'd hate to feel like this if I'm well."

Funny Stuff

Two friends met each other in front of the psychiatrist's office.

"Hello," said the first, "are you coming or going?"

The friend replied, "If I knew that I wouldn't be here."

Ministerial Mirth

A country church had a week of revival meetings, and they were so good that they decided to extend them another week.

Then they extended them for a third week.

The fourth week of the revival the pastor was so elated that he called on some of the members to testify as to what the revival meant to them.

One person after another praised the Lord for the good revival.

The oldest woman in the church then stood and said, "It was a great revival, Pastor, and I am just full and running over."

Tommy, an eight-year-old said, "I got a belly full of it too."

◆

During a business meeting in a small southern mountain church, one of the deacons said, "Pastor, I think we need a chandelier for the church."

"No," replied another deacon. "I'm against it."

"Why don't you think we need a chandelier, Brother Deacon?" asked the pastor.

"Well, first, nobody in the church can spell it; second, nobody in the church can play it; and third, what this church needs above all else, is mo' light!"

A parishioner had dozed off to sleep during the morning service.

"Will all who want to go to heaven stand?" the preacher asked.

All stood, except the sleeping parishioner.

"Well, will all who want to go to the other place stand?" asked the preacher.

At that moment someone suddenly dropped a hymnal. Quickly the sleeping man jumped to his feet and stood sheepishly facing the preacher.

He mumbled confusedly, "Well, preacher, I don't know what we're voting for, but it looks like you and I are the only ones for it."

✦

An evangelist called a church and said, "I want to come to your church and preach."

The pastor said, "No, Joe. You are not ready."

Six months later, the evangelist called again and said, "Pastor, I really want to come and preach at your church."

The pastor said, "No, Joe. You are not ready."

Six months later, the evangelist called again and said, "Pastor, I want to come and preach at your church so much that I'll pay my way—no honorarium."

The pastor said, "Okay, Joe. You are ready."

A pastor called a congregational meeting to decide whether to repair the church building or tear it down and build a new one. Most of the brethren wanted the new church, but the decision seemed to rest upon the attitude and generosity of a wealthy deacon. When called upon to express himself, the brother arose and said: "It is true the old church is badly in need of repairs, but I think we should do that instead of building a new one. I'll subscribe fifty dollars toward repairing the old church."

The portly man, as he took his seat, jarred the building, and a piece of loose plaster fell on his head. Jumping to his feet he said: "This building is in worse shape than I thought. I'll make it five hundred for repairs."

As he took his seat again, another member was heard to mutter a prayer: "Oh, Lord, hit him again!"

✦

A little old lady got into an argument with her pastor. The pastor thought he would never see her again. However she showed up for the evening service the same Sunday.

"I thought you'd gone for good," he said to her.

"Pastor," she said, "I'm going to be loyal to my church, even if the devil is in the pulpit."

A lady gave her pastor an apple pie.

He took it home, cut it, took a bite, and immediately spit it out. It was so terrible he threw it out the window.

The next Sunday the lady who gave him the pie was the first in line to greet him. She said, "How did you like the pie?"

Cheerfully, he replied, "I tell you a pie like that doesn't stay around our house very long."

◆

A minister's son said, "My daddy can take the same text and preach a different sermon every Sunday."

The other minister's son said, "Yeah? That's nothing. My daddy can take a different text every Sunday and preach the same sermon."

◆

A preacher who suffered extremely strained relations with his congregation was finally appointed chaplain at the state prison. Elated to be rid of him so easily, the people came in great numbers to hear his farewell discourse.

The pastor chose as his text: "I go and prepare a place for you. . .that where I am, there ye may be also." (John 14:3)

A pastor got carried away in his sermon and preached for two hours, with no sign of ending.

One of the members got up to leave and the pastor said, "Brother Smith, where are you going?"

"I'm going to get a haircut," Brother Smith replied.

The pastor said, "Why didn't you get one before you came?"

"I didn't need one then," replied Brother Smith.

♦

The front door of Murphy's house was badly warped, causing the door to jam now and then. To pry it open they kept a hatchet handy.

One day the doorbell rang. Murphy himself peeked out through the curtains and then shouted in a voice that could be heard through three doors: "Quick, Tommy. It's the pastor. Get the hatchet!"

♦

A church whose members could never agree on anything had its pastor taken ill and rushed to the hospital.

The chairman of the deacons visited him and said, "We voted seven to five in our deacons' meeting to pray for you."

A new preacher preached a sermon in Kentucky against tobacco.

A deacon said, "Pastor, Kentucky is the heart of tobacco country."

The minister prepared a sermon on the evils of whiskey. Another deacon noted that Kentucky was famous for its whiskey.

Next, the pastor preached a sermon on the evils of horse racing. "Pastor, maybe you didn't know it, but horse racing is also very popular in Kentucky."

"Well, what can I preach on then?" the pastor asked.

"Son," said the deacon, "Why don't you preach on witch doctors? There is not one in a thousand miles of here."

◆

A mountain church wanted its pastor to have a Doctor of Divinity degree.

The pastor found a school that would give a D.D. for $250. The congregation tried and tried to raise the money but could raise only $125.

"Well, there's only one thing to do. Let's write the school to send our pastor one D and we'll get the other one later."

A pastor visited a family who had not attended church for some time.

After the pastor had asked the husband why they had not attended church recently, he replied, "Well, pastor, I have been out of work, all the kids have been sick, and it has rained so much."

"But," the pastor replied, "it's always dry in the church."

"Yep," replied the husband, "and that's another reason."

A young pastor finally got up enough courage to ask the richest member of his church why he always fell asleep when he was preaching.

And the man replied, "Look, pastor, would I fall asleep if I didn't trust you?"

A pulpit committee was interviewing a prospective pastor.

"Preacher, we want a pastor that will stay a while. So many of our pastors don't stay very long," the chairman remarked.

"Folks, I'm your man," he replied. "I stayed with the last two churches until they both died."

Funny Stuff

A minister was to play golf with a church member when it started to rain just before the game.

The parishioner said to his pastor, "See if you can pull some strings upstairs. You have connections, don't you?"

"Friend," said the pastor, "that's management and I'm only sales."

◆

"How many members do you have in your church?" a friend of the pastor inquired.

"Three hundred and fifty," replied the pastor.

"Are all of them active?" asked the friend.

"Yes," replied the pastor. "One hundred seventy-five are working for me, and the other one hundred and seventy-five are working against me."

◆

A minister asked a man why he didn't come to church.

The man said, "Preacher, the first time I attended church, they dunked me in the water, the second time I attended, you tied me to a wife that I've had ever since."

And the minister said, "And the next time you come, we'll throw dirt on you."

The Prodigal Son was the subject of the Sunday school lesson and the minister, who had paused to visit the children's class, was dwelling on the character of the elder brother.

"But amidst all the enjoyment," said the preacher, "there was one to whom the preparation of the feast brought no joy, to whom the prodigal's return gave no happiness, only bitterness; one who did not approve of the feast and had no wish to attend it. Now who can tell me who this was?"

Silence for several moments; then a hand rose and a small sympathetic voice said, "Please, pastor, was it the fatted calf?"

◆

He was seriously ill and called for the pastor. "Pastor, if you pray for me to recover and I do, I will give you twenty-five thousand dollars toward the new church you are building."

The pastor prayed and the man got well. Although the pastor tried tactfully to remind him of his pledge, it met with no success. Finally, he frankly told him: "You promised to give twenty-five thousand dollars for the new church."

"Did I?" said the recovered man. "Well, that should give you some idea of how sick I really was."

An elderly lady had a parrot that was using offensive language. Every time the lady would come into the room it would say, "I wish she were dead. I wish she were dead."

She told her pastor about it and he said, "I have a parrot, too, but it is never rude. You bring your parrot over and leave it for several weeks, and maybe it will take up my parrot's good behavior."

So she did. Returning for it after a time she opened the door and walked in. Her parrot saw her and said, "I wish she were dead." Then the minister's parrot chimed in and said, "Amen, Lord, grant her request."

◆

A young minister was called to his first church, a small rural West Virginia mountain parish.

He heard immediately that they kept a minister only one year, but after his first year was up, they informed him that they desired him to stay another year.

He was dumbfounded and asked why they had decided to continue his services.

"Well, we don't like no preacher at all, but we find that you are nearer that than any other one we have had."

A pastor and a deacon visited a house to call on a prospect.

They knocked, and a small voice said, "Come in."

They went in but no one was there, except two big Doberman dogs, poised to attack them.

They said, "Hello, is anyone here?" and the voice of the little old lady said, "Come in."

It sounded like it was coming from the kitchen, so they went that direction. There was a parrot saying, "Come in, come in, come in. . ."

The pastor said, "You silly old parrot, is that all you can say?"

With the same small voice the parrot said, "Sic 'em."

✦

A hat was passed around a certain congregation for the purpose of taking up an offering for the visiting minister.

Presently it was returned to him—emphatically and embarrassingly empty. Slowly and deliberately, the parson inverted the hat and shook it meaningfully. Then, raising his eyes to heaven, he exclaimed fervently: "I thank Thee, dear Lord, that I got my hat back from this congregation."

A minister was so dry that the people were all dozing after his one-hour sermon.

So he took a songbook and waved it to attract their attention, but suddenly he dropped it and it fell on the head of an old man.

He opened his eyes slightly and said, "Hit me again. I can still hear him."

The Lumbermen's Association and the Baptist preachers held their meeting in the same hotel in Chicago.

The ministers were to be served apple pie and ice cream and the lumbermen were to be served watermelon and rum.

However, the waiters got the menus mixed up and served the ministers the watermelon and rum.

As the head waiter discovered the error, he called the waiters and excitedly asked them if they had served the ministers the watermelon and rum.

"Yes," they replied.

"Did they eat it?" he asked.

"Yes," they replied.

"Well, what did they say?" he inquired.

"Oh, they didn't say anything, but they did put the seeds in their pockets."

The new minister found only one person at this first rural Sunday night service. "What do you think we should do about the service," he asked the man, "inasmuch as we have such a small congregation?"

The man replied, "Well, sir, I have never been to school very much. I don't have much education and I don't know much about the Bible, but this one thing I know, that when I promise my cows a load of hay, I always keep my promise."

"Well, come in then, and we will have a service," said the minister. The minister was long-winded, and it was an exceptionally long service. Afterward the minister asked the farmer, "What did you think of the service?"

"Well," he said, "I have never been to school, I'm not educated, and I don't know much about the Bible, but this one thing I know, when I promise my cows a load of hay and only one shows up, I never give it the whole load."

✦

A young son asked his dad, "How come our pastor gets three weeks vacation, and you get only one week?"

"Well, Son," he replied, "if he's a good minister, he needs a good vacation, and if he isn't a good minister, his congregation needs it."

Funny Stuff

It was announced in church one day that a substitute preacher would preach.

A little boy leaned over and asked his mother, "What is a substitute?"

"Well, for example, Son, if you threw your baseball through the window and broke it, and we didn't have another real pane, we could put a piece of cardboard in the window. . .that's what we call a substitute."

When the substitute minister had finished preaching that morning, the little boy leaned over and said, "Mother, this sure isn't a substitute. . .he's a real pain!"

◆

A revival was being conducted by a muscular preacher. He was disturbed by several young men who scoffed at everything they saw or heard.

He paused and asked them why they attended the meeting. "We came to see a miracle performed," impudently replied one of them.

Leaving the pulpit and walking quietly down the aisle, the minister seized one after the other by the collar, and as they disappeared out of the door, remarked: "We don't perform miracles here, but we do cast out demons!"

A minister's wife told her husband never to open a box she had in her closet.

But he couldn't resist, so one day after many years, he opened it while she was out shopping.

He found three eggs, and a big pile of money—at least $3,000.

When the wife returned, he said, "I'm sorry, honey, but curiosity got the best of me and I opened the box. What about those three eggs in there?"

She said, "Well, every time you preached a bad sermon, I put one egg in the box."

"Well, that's not too bad—three bad sermons in twenty years. That's pretty good. And where did you get all that money?" he asked.

She replied, "Every time I got a dozen eggs, I sold them."

◆

"Daddy," said the little girl as she watched her father, a minister, struggle with his next Sunday sermon, "doesn't God tell you what to say?"

"Of course, He does, honey," the father said.

"They why do you keep scratching out some of the words?"

Funny Stuff

The minister's wife held a garden party and, through an oversight, forgot to invite one little old lady who had been a member of the church since it was built. The party was well in progress in the sunny garden when the minister's wife suddenly remembered the old lady. She excused herself from the guests and ran in to the telephone. "Oh, Mrs. Flibberty," she exclaimed in an apologetic tone, "we wouldn't dream of omitting you deliberately. Please come on out!"

"Oh no, it's too late now," crackled the little old voice on the other end of the line.

"Why too late?" said the minister's wife. "I can send a car for you!"

"No, no, it's too late," the old voice repeated. "I've already prayed for rain."

He had been around from church to church, trying to find a congenial congregation. Finally, he stopped in a little church just as the congregation read with the minister: "We have left undone those things which we ought to have done."

The man dropped into a pew with a sigh of relief. "Thank goodness," he observed. "I've found my crowd at last."

There was a rich oilman who was getting married and was nervous about it. He told the minister that the fee would be in proportion to the brevity of the service and that if he used a long service he wouldn't receive a cent.

When the wedding day came, the couple stood before the minister in the bride's home. The minister said to the man "Take her?" and to the woman, "Take him?" and then closed the ceremony by announcing, "Took."

◆

After their cars had collided, two women began arguing about who was at fault.

One of them said, "My husband is a minister. What do you think he will say?"

The other woman responded, "Well, my husband isn't a minister. What do you think he will say?"

◆

The janitor had dropped a box of tacks in the pulpit of the church.

"Now what if you should miss picking up all of those tacks and I should step on one during my sermon?" the aggravated minister asked.

"Sir," replied the janitor, "I bet that's one point you wouldn't linger on."

A pastor was called and asked to visit an old man who lived quite a way out of town.

The wife, doing the calling, said, "Pastor, I hate to ask you to come so far, but my husband is very sick."

"Oh, that's quite all right," he replied. "I have another parishioner in the neighborhood, so I'll just come out and kill two birds with one stone."

✦

A preacher had only two hand gestures. For one, his hand would point up, and for the other, his hand would point down.

As he was preaching one day he raised his arm and pointed upward and said, "When the roll is called up yonder."

Then he lowered his arms and pointed down, and said, "I'll be there."

✦

A man told his boss he was called to be a preacher and resigned his job.

But he was back on the job in two weeks.

"I thought you were called by God to preach," he was asked.

"Yes, but that was before He heard me preach," he replied.

I got pulled over by policeman. "Please don't give me a ticket, I'm just a poor preacher," I said.

"I know," said the policeman. "I heard you preach last night."

✦

A preacher was called to give a trial sermon. After he had preached he made his way out of the church so the church could vote on him.

On his way down the aisle he kicked a boy's dog, and said, "Get out of here, you mongrel."

Everybody saw what he had done, so they followed him out of the church and formed a circle around him.

A deacon said, "Brother preacher, I want to thank you for running that dog out of the church."

The preacher said, "You want to thank me? Why?"

The deacon said, "I wouldn't have my dog hear that sermon for anything in the world."

✦

A preacher was quoting a verse about visiting the sick, raising the dead, and casting out devils. He got a little mixed up and said: "The Bible admonishes us to cast out the sick. . .heal the dead. . .and raise the devil."

The train robber went from car to car, holding up the passengers and taking their money and jewelry.

Eventually he came to the last man, who said, "You wouldn't rob a preacher, would you?"

"What kind of a preacher are you?" the robber asked.

"I'm a Presbyterian."

The robber took the gun in his left hand, held out his right hand, and said, "Put it there, brother. I'm one, too."

◆

A little boy, after attending Sunday school, was asked what he learned.

"We heard about a man named Moses. He went behind the lines and rescued the Israelites. Then he came to the Red Sea, and called his engineers and they built a pontoon bridge. After they got across, he saw the enemy tanks approaching, so he got on his walkie-talkie and called headquarters, and they sent the dive bombers and blew up the bridge. Then the Israelites rode on."

"Now, Son, it wasn't like that at all, was it?"

"Well, not exactly. But if I told you how the teacher said it really happened, you wouldn't have believed it either!"

A Good Will Team composed of a Catholic priest, a Methodist minister, and a Jewish rabbi was about to begin its meeting in the Methodist church of a small Kansas town. They agreed to use a startling and shocking trick to get attention.

The priest arose and announced: "I pray all Protestants would move out of town."

The minister followed suit: "I pray all Catholics would move out of town."

The rabbi followed: "I pray you would both have your prayer granted."

✦

A little boy in Sunday school was asked what commandment would he break if he stayed home from Sunday school. He replied, "The third one: Keep the Sabbath day holy."

Then he was asked what commandment he would break if he took John's bicycle home with him. He replied, "The seventh: Thou shalt not steal."

Then he was asked what commandment he would break if he pulled John's dog's tail. He hesitated, and said "I don't know the number, but it goes like this: 'What God has joined together, let no man pull apart.'"

A clergyman was spending the afternoon at a house in the English village where he had preached. After tea he was sitting in the garden with his hostess. Out rushed her little boy holding a rat above his head.

"Don't be afraid, Mother," he cried, "it's dead. We beat him and bashed him and thumped him until. . ." Then, catching sight of the clergyman he added in a lowered voice, ". . .until God called him home."

A couple was touring the Capitol in Washington, and the guide pointed to a tall, benevolent gentleman as the congressional chaplain.

The lady asked, "What does the chaplain do? Does he pray for the Senate or the House?"

The guide answered, "Neither. He gets up, looks at the Congress, and then prays for the country."

The rabbi was asked, "This is a very poor synagogue. How much do they pay you?"

"Ten dollars a month."

"How can you live on that?"

"I'm lucky that I'm a very religious man. If I didn't fast three times a week, I'd starve to death."

The bishop was addressing the Sunday school. In his most expressive tones, he was saying: "And now, children, let me tell you a very sad fact. In Africa, there are ten million square miles of territory and hardly any Sunday schools where little boys and girls can spend their Sundays. Now, what should we all try to save up our money and do?"

"Go to Africa!" was the unanimous reply.

"My dear young lady," said the clergyman, in grieved tones as he listened to an extremely modern young woman tear off some of the very latest jazz on the piano, "have you ever heard of 'The Ten Commandments'?"

"Whistle a few bars," said the young lady, "and I think I can follow you."

A Baptist family had a death in the family while their minister was out of town.

They asked the local Methodist minister to conduct the funeral service. He said he would have to check with the bishop. He sent an e-mail to the bishop asking, "Could I bury a Baptist?"

The bishop replied, "Sure. Bury all the Baptists you can!"

Little Billy came home from Sunday school all excited. "Grandma, did you ever hear the story of the good American?"

"No," she said. "Do tell me, honey."

"Well," spouted Billy, "there was this salesman who was traveling from Jerusalem to Jericho. Some bad guys mugged him. They beat him up and almost killed him. Lots of people walked right by but didn't help the guy. Then a 'Good American' saw him, stopped his Mustang, gave the guy some money, and took him to a motel."

Two brothers were known as the two most horrible men that had ever lived.

When one of them died, the other said to the minister, "If you will preach my brother's funeral and call him a saint, I'll give you a thousand dollars."

The minister agreed to do it.

The minister, standing beside the casket, said, "This man was a dope fiend, a murderer, a thief, and a terrible scoundrel, but compared to this man standing beside him, he was a saint."

A Texan who raised horses visited South Florida for his vacation.

He saw a race track advertised and decided to visit it. He had never gambled, but he just wanted to see the horses run.

However, he noticed a Catholic priest blessing the horses before they ran in the race, and every one he blessed won.

He thought, *I know gambling is wrong, but this is not gambling—it's a sure thing.* So, he bet on the last horse that the priest had blessed.

The horse started the race well, but ran slower and slower until at the finish line it fell dead.

The Texan confronted the priest and said, "Father, I don't understand. You blessed four horses and they all won, but the fifth one—I bet on him and he not only lost, but fell dead. How do you explain that?"

The priest said, "I can tell you are not a Catholic, sir, for if you were you would know the difference between a blessing and a last rite."

Funny Stuff

A Baptist deacon had advertised a cow for sale.

"How much are you asking for it?" inquired a prospective purchaser.

"A hundred and fifty dollars," said the advertiser.

"And how much milk does she give?"

"Four gallons a day," he replied.

"But how do I know that she will actually give that amount?" asked the purchaser.

"Oh, you can trust me," reassured the advertiser, "I'm a Baptist deacon."

"I'll buy it," replied the other. "I'll take the cow home and bring you back the money later. You can trust me, I'm a Presbyterian elder."

When the deacon arrived home he asked his wife, "What is a Presbyterian elder?"

"Oh," she explained, "a Presbyterian elder is about the same as a Baptist deacon."

"Oh, dear," groaned the deacon, "I have lost my cow!"

A young man was asked to preach just before the morning service at a Bible conference. The regular speaker had not shown up for the service.

This young man was scared to death. He wasn't prepared and didn't know what to say.

He went to the bishop's tent and said, "What will I do? I have no sermon. What will I do?"

The bishop said, "Trust in the Lord, Son, trust in the Lord."

In desperation, he picked up the bishop's Bible and found a nice set of typewritten notes, so he took them and preached the bishop's sermon.

Everyone was amazed. The people crowded around him and told him what a great sermon it was.

Then came the bishop, "Young man," he said, "you preached my sermon—the one I had prepared for tonight. What am I going to do tonight?"

With much dignity, the young man replied, "Trust in the Lord, bishop, just trust the Lord."

A newly graduated seminary student wanted his first sermon to be the best, so he studied and prepared for days.

His topic was about Jesus' feeding the five thousand. Everything went perfectly during the service and it was time for his message.

During this message, he became confused and said, "Jesus took the five thousand loaves and two thousand fishes and fed the five. Now that's a miracle! Could you do that?"

An old deacon in the front nodded that he could.

The young preacher was furious, so after the service, he stopped the deacon and said, "Now, how could you perform that miracle?"

The deacon explained the mistake he had made in his numbers. The young preacher tried to find a way to cover his mistake in his next sermon. The more he thought the more confused he became, so he decided to meet his mistake head-on and preach the next Sunday on the same subject.

The next Sunday morning he got it all together and preached it correctly. Jesus took the five loaves and two fish and fed the five thousand. Then he said, "Could any of you do that?" The old deacon nodded yes again.

The young preacher was really furious this

time. After the service he buttonholed the deacon again. "Now, how in the world could you feed five thousand with five loaves and two fish?"

"Well," the old deacon exclaimed, "I'd just use what I had left over from last Sunday."

Miscellaneous
Mirth

The lecturer was illustrating the evils of liquor. Producing two glasses, one filled with water and the other with whiskey, he proceeded to drop a live worm into each glass. The worm in the water swam around in a lively manner, while the one in the whiskey promptly curled up and died.

"Now then," he exclaimed triumphantly, "what does this prove?"

A woman answered from the back row: "If you drink whiskey, you won't have worms."

The beggar was dirty and hungry and as the old lady passed by she gave him five cents. "Tell me," she said, "how did you get so destitute?"

"Well, ma'am," the old beggar said, "I was like you at one time, always giving vast sums to the poor."

"There I was—a bull coming at me in one direction and a bear in the other. And I only had one shell."

"Well, which did you shoot?"

"I shot the bear."

"Why?"

"Well, I could shoot the bull anytime."

A lady took her cat to the veterinarian.

The vet immediately gave it a little green pill. He then turned the cat on its back on the table and checked its stomach. Then he put it on its stomach and checked its back. Then he checked on both sides.

"Your cat is fine," the vet then said. "Everything is okay."

"Thank you, doctor—what is the charge?"

"Three hundred fifty-three dollars," said the veterinarian.

"Doc, don't you think that's a little high?" she asked.

"No," said the vet. "It was $3.00 for the pill and $350.00 for the CAT scan."

An eighteen-year-old soldier was given guard duty one night. He did his best for a while, but in the early morning he went to sleep. He awakened to find his superior standing over him.

Remembering the heavy penalty for being asleep on guard duty, this smart-thinking young man kept his head bowed for another moment, then looked piously upward and reverently intoned, "A-a-a-a-men!"

A riverboat captain, trying to calm his passengers, said, "I've been running boats on this river for so long I know where every sandbar is."

Suddenly the boat struck a sandbar so hard all were shaken. "See," he said, "there's one of them now."

✦

A man went to the bus station to catch a bus, but found he was early. He saw a little fortune-telling machine and decided to put a nickel in the slot. A little card came out that said, "You are John Jones—you are sixty-five years old—you are on your way to Chicago on a business trip."

He said, "I don't believe this machine knows this information. There must be someone behind it." But he put another nickel in and another card came out saying, "You are John Jones—you are sixty-five years old—you are on your way to Chicago on a business trip."

"I just don't believe it," said the man again, as he put in another nickel. This time a card came out saying: "You are still John Jones—you are still sixty-five years old—you are still on your way to Chicago—but you've fooled around and missed your bus."

A big executive boarded a New York to Chicago train. He explained to the porter, "I'm a heavy sleeper and I want you to be sure and wake me at 3 A.M. to get off in Buffalo. Regardless of what I say, get me up, for I have some important business there."

The next morning the executive awakened in Chicago. He found the porter and sternly reprimanded him.

After the man had left, someone asked the porter, "How could you stand there and take that kind of talk from that man?"

The porter explained: "That ain't nothing. You should've heard what the man said that I did put off at Buffalo."

✦

An alumnus was asked to return to Yale and give a speech.

He said, "I'm going to speak on four simple letters—Y-A-L-E."

For about thirty minutes he spoke on youth. Then, thirty minutes on ambition, then thirty on loyalty, and finally thirty on energy.

A student was asked how he liked the lecture.

"Fine, but I'm sure glad he wasn't speaking at the Massachusetts Institute of Technology."

A foreigner stopped for lunch in a small town and noticing he was opposite a college, decided to take a look at the place. As he passed a student on the campus, he stopped the lad and asked the name of the school.

"Sorry, sir, I really don't know," he muttered. "I'm just a football player here."

◆

The pet shop delivery boy was not exactly the brightest lad in the world. One day he was asked to deliver a pet rabbit to "Mrs. Jones, Route 2, Box 4."

"You had better write that down in case I forget it," said the boy.

Slipping the address into his pocket he started off on his errand. Every few minutes he glanced at the address and said, "I know where I'm going. Mrs. Jones, Route 2, Box 4."

Everything went smoothly until he hit a crater in the road. The truck he was driving landed in a ditch and the rabbit began to run for its life across an open field.

The boy stood there laughing uproariously. When asked by a passerby what was so funny, he said, "Did you see that crazy rabbit running across the field? He doesn't know where he's going because I've got the address in my pocket."

A fellow took his first plane ride. He had to be coaxed to get on. And when he got on, fortunately there was one seat. Unfortunately, it was by the window. Fortunately, the plane got airborne. Unfortunately, it developed engine trouble. Fortunately, there was a parachute. Unfortunately, it didn't open. Fortunately, there was this huge haystack down below. Unfortunately, there was a pitchfork with the business end of it sticking straight up. Fortunately, he missed the pitchfork. Unfortunately, he missed the haystack.

A Kentucky boy was boasting to a visiting Texan about the gold in Fort Knox.

"Here in Kentucky," he said, "we've enough gold to build a sold gold fence, three feet high and two feet wide, all the way around Texas."

"Well, go ahead and build it," said the Texan. "If we like it, we'll buy it."

The woman was filling out an accident report, and she wrote as follows: "I had to back out of the driveway, and by the time I had backed out far enough to see what was coming, it already had."

A man told his friend that he never ate cake, pie, or candy. Nor did he ever eat food with additives, or anything that had been sprayed, or anything that had been biologically engineered.

"Well, how do you feel?" his friend asked.

He replied, "Hungry."

✦

A rich Texan suddenly clutched his heart and yelled at his wife: "I think I'm gonna have an attack. Well, don't just stand there, girl. Buy me a hospital."

✦

The crime situation is terrible. A gunman rushed out of a movie one day, stuck his gun into the cashier's cage and said, "I didn't like the movie. Give me everybody's money back."

✦

A lady was drowning and a man jumped in and grabbed her by the hair, but she wore a wig and it came off.

Then he grabbed her by the chin, and her false teeth came out.

The man shouted, "Somebody help me save all of this woman that we can."

Funny Stuff

A class of students was watching the professor of chemistry give a demonstration of the properties of various acids. "Now," said the professor, "I am going to drop a half-dollar into this glass of acid. Will it dissolve?"

"No sir," replied one of the students.

"No?" said the professor. "Then perhaps you will explain to the class why it won't dissolve."

"Because," came the answer, "if the money would dissolve, you wouldn't drop it in."

Joe was having trouble getting up in the mornings, so his doctor prescribed some pills. Joe took them, slept well, and was awake before the alarm rang.

He took his time getting to the office, strolled in, and said to his boss, "I didn't have a bit of trouble getting up this morning."

"That's great," replied the boss. "But where were you yesterday?"

An ad in a country newspaper read: Handsome and intelligent farmer wishes to meet a young woman who owns a tractor. Please write soon and enclose a picture of the tractor.

John had been convicted and sentenced to death. The last day of his life had come. The warden awakened him and asked him what he would have for breakfast. "Since it's your last day, John, you can have anything you want."

"Thank you. I reckon I'll just take watermelon."

"But this is December! Watermelons aren't planted yet, much less ripe."

"I can wait."

✦

A traveler stopped at a historic old hotel and asked the clerk for the nightly rate for a single room.

"A room on the first floor is fifty dollars; on the second floor, forty dollars; and on the third floor, thirty dollars," answered the clerk.

The man looked around and then turned to go.

"Don't you find the hotel attractive?" asked the clerk.

"Oh, it's beautiful—it just isn't tall enough."

✦

Someone said about his condominium, "I'm surprised how thin the walls are when you are trying to sleep, and how thick they are when you are trying to listen."

During a Police Academy class, one of the questions asked began, "If you were called to a terrible automobile wreck, where you discovered the chief of police dead in one car with a bottle of booze beside him and the mayor injured in the other car, with a package of marijuana in his hand. . .

"Then suddenly you looked up to the top floor of a high-rise building across the street and saw a man on the balcony rail, ready to jump. . .

"Then you looked down the street as several fire trucks were desperately fighting a fire in the city courthouse. . ."

The instructor concluded, "My question is, what would you do under these circumstances?"

One of the new recruits, after deep contemplation said, "I'd remove my uniform and mingle with the crowd."

◆

A night watchman heard noises in the dark warehouse. Drawing his revolver, he went to the door and called: "Come out with your hands up, so I can see who you are. If you don't, I'll come in and see who you were."

There were four people on an airplane, the pilot, a computer technician, a minister, and a Boy Scout. However, there were only three parachutes on board the plane.

Suddenly, the plane developed motor trouble and it began to fall fast.

The pilot immediately grabbed the first parachute and said, "I'm the most important man on this airplane and I must go and report this accident." He waved and jumped out.

The computer technician said, "I'm the smartest man in the world, and I'm working on a project that will benefit all mankind. It would be a tragedy if I were killed." He grabbed a pack, waved, and jumped.

The minister said, "There's only one parachute left, so Son, you go ahead and use it. I'm an old man, I've lived a good life, and I'm ready to die. Go ahead, Son, and jump."

The Boy Scout said, "Sir, that won't be necessary. We can both jump, for there are still two parachutes left. You see, sir, the smartest man in the world just jumped out with my backpack."

Among other things, a first-grade teacher told her charges that nowadays more twins are born than in past years. One little fellow asked: "Why is that?" Before the teacher could attempt an answer, another little fellow spoke up: "Because these days little children are afraid to come into the world alone."

◆

A ragged, hungry hobo stopped a well-dressed rich man on the street and asked him for money for food. "I'll do better than that," said the rich man. "Come into the bar and I'll buy you a drink."

"Thank you, sir," said the beggar, "but I'm not a drinking man."

"Well, then have a cigar," offered the rich man.

"No, thanks. I don't smoke."

"Okay," said the rich man. "I'll make a bet for you on a horse that's absolutely guaranteed to win, and you'll collect enough cash for plenty of food and a new suit besides."

"Please, no," said the hobo. "I only need a bite, just a bite."

"Well, then," said the rich man, "how would you like to come home with me to dinner? I want my wife to see for herself what happens to a guy who doesn't smoke, drink, or gamble."

An old mountaineer bought a chain saw at the hardware store. The clerk explained that he could saw five cords of wood a day with it. As a matter of fact, it was guaranteed to saw five cords.

The old mountaineer went out the first day, and he worked hard, but only got one cord. He came in and told his wife that something was wrong. She said, "Go out early and stay late, and maybe you can get five cords."

He got up before sunup, didn't take time to eat, and worked until it was dark, but he didn't get but two cords. He was so tired he went straight to bed. His wife said, "I'd take that thing back to the store in the morning."

The next morning he confronted the salesman and complained, "You said I could saw five cords with this saw, and I only got two. Something is wrong."

The salesman said, "Well, now, let me check it."

He took the handle on the rope in his hand and pulled the cord. The motor started.

The old mountaineer jumped back and said, "What's that noise?"

The new maid answered the phone, "Yes, you are right," she said, and hung up the receiver.

Again the phone rang and she answered, "Yes, ma'am, it sure is!" and hung up again.

"Who was that?" asked her mistress.

"I don't know, ma'am," replied the maid. "Some crazy lady kept saying, 'It's a long distance call from New York,' and I said, 'It sure is.' "

◆

A man, talking to a friend from another city, said, "Man, I wouldn't want to live in your city with all that crime you have down there—the drugs, murder, and robbery."

"Oh, I don't know about that," said the friend. "I live there and I don't think it's so bad."

"By the way, what are you doing for a living these days?" the first man asked.

"I'm a tail gunner on a milk truck," he replied.

◆

When the traffic cop stopped the motorist, she asked indignantly, "What do you want with me?"

"You were traveling seventy miles per hour," answered the police officer.

"Seventy miles an hour? Why, I haven't even been driving an hour," protested the woman.

A driver tucked this note under the windshield wiper of his automobile: "I've circled the block for twenty minutes. I'm late for an appointment, and if I don't park here I'll lose my job. 'Forgive us our trespasses.' "

When he came back he found a parking ticket and this note: "I've circled the block for twenty years, and if I don't give you a ticket, I'll lose my job. 'Lead us not into temptation.' "

One afternoon a well-dressed lady stopped at the gates of a mental institution.

"I wonder," she asked, "if you could tell me who's responsible for this magnificent garden? I'd like to hire the gardener."

"I am," said the patient. "I've been cured a very long time," he pointed out, "but no one from the out-side will give me a job, so they just keep me here."

"That's foolish," said the dowager. "You're no more unbalanced than I am. I'm going to talk to the doctor in charge, and I'll have you out of here in no time."

Just as she reached her car, she felt a violent blow to her head as someone hit her with a stone. Turning around, half-stunned, she saw the gardener smiling at her.

"Now you won't forget," he called out, "will you?"

Funny Stuff

A little boy was given the opportunity to ride on top of a stagecoach with the driver.

He watched the driver as he used his whip. He could knock a horsefly off the back of a horse. He could knock a twig off a tree limb.

Suddenly the boy saw a large hornet's nest on a tree limb. The boy said, "Let me see you hit it."

The driver said, "No lad, I ain't gonna mess with them—they're organized."

With all the problems of prayer in school the teachers are rather nervous.

A little group of boys was caught shooting dice.

The teacher came in the room and said "What are you boys doing?"

Shooting dice, they admitted. "Thank goodness," the teacher said. "For a minute I thought you were praying."

A woman was in a store to buy a toaster.

The high-pressure salesman decided to sell her an expensive freezer instead.

"Madam, believe me when I tell you this freezer will pay for itself in no time at all."

"Fine. As soon as it does, send it over."

A little prospector wearing clean new shoes walked into a saloon. A big Texan said to his friend standing at the bar, "Watch me make this dude dance." He walked over to the prospector and said, "You're a foreigner, aren't you? From the East?"

"You might say that," the little prospector answered. "I'm from Boston and I'm here prospecting for gold."

"Now tell me something. Can you dance?"

"No, sir. I never did learn to dance."

"Well, I'm going to teach you. You'll be surprised how quickly you can learn."

With that, the Texan took out his gun and started shooting at the prospector's feet. Hopping, skipping, jumping, by the time the little prospector made it to the door, he was shaking like a leaf.

About an hour later the Texan left the saloon. As soon as he stepped outside the door, he heard a click. He looked around and there, four feet from his head, was the biggest shotgun he had ever seen.

And the little prospector said, "Mr. Texan, have you ever kissed a mule?"

"No," said the quick-thinking Texan, "but I've always wanted to."

A football team in a small school had an outstanding player by the name of Stonewall. As a matter of fact he was "the" team. My, how he could carry the ball.

The team finally met a team with a strong defense. Their backfield was known as the Stone Wall.

The quarterback centered the ball, and the receiver went wide to the left, but was knocked down with no gain. The coach cried, "Give the ball to Stonewall." The crowd screamed, "Give the ball to Stonewall."

The next play the quarterback gave the ball to a receiver who went far to the right, but was flattened by eleven players. The coach yelled, "Give the ball to Stonewall." The crowd yelled, "Give the ball to Stonewall."

After the next similar disastrous play, the coach yelled to the quarterback, "I said, give the ball to Stonewall."

The quarterback looked up from the ball and cried back, "Coach, Stonewall don't want the ball."

She: "This is an ideal spot for a picnic."
He: "It must be. Fifty million insects can't be wrong."

A young man from Kentucky was vacationing in Washington, D.C. He decided to call upon one of the senators from the Bluegrass State. As it was late afternoon the young man invited the congressman out to dinner, asking him to suggest a high-class restaurant. As they were ordering, the young man said: "Boy, I'd like to have a steak smothered in onions, but I'm supposed to meet my girlfriend and her mother tonight and they wouldn't like the smell of onions on my breath."

"Oh, don't worry," assured the senator, "order the steak and onions. When you get the bill it will take your breath away."

◆

Two fellows met on the street. One said to the other, "Say, I haven't seen you for five years. What have you been doing?"

The other replied softly, "Five years."

◆

After the rifle tournament was completed, one young army recruit was very discouraged by his poor showing. As he turned in his card to the top sergeant, he remarked: "What a score! I feel like shooting myself!"

"Well," replied the sergeant sympathetically, after looking over the card, "you'd better take two bullets."

A pretty circus girl, all dressed up in an evening dress, would hold a marshmallow in her mouth, while one of the lions in the cage would jump up and take it out of her mouth.

Some hecklers yelled, "So, what? That's no big deal."

The manager said, "Would one of you brave boys like to try it?"

One of the hecklers yelled, "Sure I would, if you took those crazy lions out of there."

A man often walked through a cemetery, since it was a shortcut, on his way home. One night he stumbled and fell into a new grave. For almost an hour he tried to get out of the deep hole, but finally he gave up and settled down for the night.

A farmer out possum hunting came walking through and he, too, fell into the grave. He began a desperate attempt to get out, unaware there was anyone else in the grave.

The first man listened to him silently for a few minutes, then reached over in the pitch darkness and laid a hand on his shoulder. "You can't get out of here."

But the farmer did.

A man was asked by his friend, a college coach, to help him to get some good new football players.

"Coach, I know what kind of player you want," he said. "You don't want the player that when he gets knocked down, stays down, do you, coach?"

"No," said the coach.

"And you don't want the player who gets knocked down, but finally gets up, do you, coach?"

"No," said the coach.

"But, I know you want the player that when he gets knocked down, he gets up—knock him down and he gets up every time."

"No," said the coach.

"You don't want the guy who gets up every time he is knocked down—why, coach?"

"Listen, friend, I want that guy that is knocking everybody else down," said the coach.

✦

A foreign diplomat once came in upon Abraham Lincoln while he was blacking his shoes.

"What, Mr. President, you black your own shoes?" the diplomat asked incredulously.

"Yes," Lincoln answered, "whose do you think I black?"

The mother said, "Son, it's time to get up and go to school."

"Mother, nobody likes me in school. The teachers don't like me. The kids don't like me. The superintendent wants to transfer me. The bus drivers hate me. The school board wants me to quit, and I don't want to go to school."

Mother said, "Son, you must go to school. You are healthy, you have a lot to learn, a lot to teach others. Son, you are a leader. And besides, Son," she added, "you're forty-five years old, and you're the principal."

A man in Birmingham liked his liquor and was a regular customer at the local pub every Saturday night.

His three sons were concerned about his drinking, and decided to try to frighten him in the hope that he would quit drinking.

So they went to the cemetery that their father passed through every Saturday night, and when he came, they appeared from behind three tombstones with sheets over their bodies.

The father murmured, "Well, if this is the resurrection, it's sure a poor showing for Birmingham."

"London," said one traveler, "is the foggiest place in the world."

"Oh no, it's not," said the other. "I've been in a place much foggier than London."

"Where was that?" asked his friend.

"I don't know where it was," replied the second man. "It was so foggy."

◆

An old man was very sick. He thought he was going to die, so he called for a Bible. "Bring it quick, I'm dying," he gasped.

Someone brought the big family Bible, with a mirror on the cover, and handed it to him.

As he looked into the mirror he cried, "Never mind. . .it's too late. . .the devil got ahead of me."

◆

Two merchants were in keen competition. One of them dreamed that an angel visited him.

"I will give you anything you want, up to a million dollars," said the angel, "if you are willing to let your competitor have double. What is your wish?"

"Angel, I wish–I wish–I wish I were blind in one eye!"

An old legend says that when the Lord created the world, He made men and all the animals to live forty years—the horse forty years, the dog forty years, and the monkey forty years.

But man was dissatisfied. He complained that this is not enough time for a man to live. So, the horse volunteered ten years of his life to go to the man's life. Then the dog said, "I'll give him ten years of mine too."

Finally, the monkey said, "I'll be a good sport. He can have ten years of mine also."

So, that's the way it is. Man lives his regular forty years and the next ten he works like a horse, the next ten he leads a dog's life, and the next ten he just monkeys around.

◆

A village blacksmith, hammering a white-hot horseshoe at his open forge, had just finished the shoe and thrown it to the ground to cool.

The local wise guy and busybody walked in at that moment. He picked up the horseshoe, but dropped it with a howl of pain.

"Pretty hot, eh?" asked the blacksmith.

"Naw," said the wise guy. "It just don't take me long to look over a horseshoe."

During a big college football game, a player called play thirteen and made a last-minute touchdown and won the game.

The coach, immediately after the game, took the player aside and said, "Why did you use play thirteen? We haven't practiced that play for months. Why did you use it?"

The player said, "I knew that whatever I did, it would be wrong, so I saw a player with eight on his back and another player with seven on his back, so I just added them together, and called play thirteen."

"Great," said the coach, "but please don't tell the newspaper about this. Seven and eight equal fifteen."

The dumb player replied, "So, if I had been as smart as you coach, we would have lost the game."

As Noah and his family were disembarking from the ark, they paused on a ridge to look back, "We should have done something, Noah," his wife said. "That old hulk of an ark will sit there and be an eyesore on the landscape for years to come."

"Everything's taken care of," Noah assured her. "I left the two termites aboard."

This tale of guile and deception was related by a Customs Inspector in San Francisco:

A little old lady was stopped as she was passing through the Customs House, and the Inspector asked her what she had in a bottle in her valise.

"Holy water," she replied in a thick Irish brogue.

The inspector uncorked the bottle and sniffed at it. "But this is Irish whiskey," he exclaimed.

"Saints be praised!" said the little old lady. "This is a miracle!"

✦

The recruit had finished his physical and was being questioned by a clerk: "Did you go to elementary school?"

The recruit snickered, "Not only elementary school," he elaborated. "I attended St. Paul's in Concord, New Hampshire, and Harvard in Cambridge, Massachusetts. I took my master's at Princeton in Princeton, New Jersey, my first Ph.D. at Oxford in England, and my second at the University of Michigan in Ann Arbor."

The clerk nodded, reached for a rubber stamp, and processed the recruit's form with one word: "Literate."

A woman angrily jumped out of her car after a collision with another car.

"Why don't people ever watch where they're driving?" she shouted wildly. "You're the fourth car I've hit today!"

✦

"What is your age?" asked the attorney in the courtroom. "Remember, madam, you are under oath."

"Twenty-nine years and some months," she replied in a loud, clear voice.

"How many months did you say?" the lawyer shouted.

She replied in very nearly a whisper, "Two hundred and fifty."

✦

Speaker: "This is terrible! I am the speaker at this banquet, and I forgot my false teeth!"

Man: "I happen to have an extra pair. Try these."

Speaker: "Too small."

Man: "Well, try this pair."

Speaker: "Too big."

Man: "I have one pair left."

Speaker: "These fit just fine. It sure is lucky to sit next to a dentist!"

Man: "I'm no dentist. I'm an undertaker."

The young convert worked as a clerk in a store operated on strictly Christian principles.

One day an elegant lady came in to buy some tapestry. Producing a roll from the lowest shelf, he said, "This is $1.98 a yard, madam."

"Young man, I can afford the very best and I want the very best," the prospective customer declared.

"Well, this is $2.98 a yard," said the clerk, producing the most expensive price range they had in fabrics.

"Young man, I don't think you understand. I want the very best!"

The clerk reached for another roll of $2.98 quality material. "We have this one at $9.98 a yard," he said.

"Fine," responded the customer, "that's just what I want!"

The owner came into the store later and was told of the transaction.

"But how can you reconcile a deal such as that with Scripture?" he asked.

Scratching his head, the young man replied, "She was a stranger and I took her in."

It had rained hard. The windshield was spattered with mud, the car had narrowly escaped several collisions, and the hitchhiker was beginning to regret that he had been picked up by this particular motorist.

"Wouldn't it be a good idea to wipe off the windshield?" he suggested anxiously.

"It wouldn't do a bit of good, Son," said the cheerful driver. "I left my glasses at home."

◆

"Don't be downhearted," said the steward to the suffering passenger. "Seasickness never killed anyone."

"Don't say that," groaned the seasick passenger. "Only the hope of dying has kept me alive this far!"

◆

They had driven and driven and driven, with nothing to break the nighttime monotony except "No Vacancy" signs on motels. And they were very sleepy people. Finally, Mother thought she would encourage Papa, who was driving. So she said, "I know we'll find a place with a vacancy soon, honey. People are starting to get up."

A man with a worried look on his face ran into a drugstore and asked the druggist if he knew a way to stop the hiccups. Without any warning the druggist slapped him in the face. Amazed and angry, the young man demanded that the druggist explain his unusual behavior.

"Well," said the druggist, "you don't have the hiccups now, do you?"

"No," answered the young man, "but my wife out in the car still does."

◆

A man riding an airplane suddenly discovered two motors on one side were on fire. He began to cry at the top of his voice, "Two motors on fire, two motors on fire."

Panic spread fast among the passengers.

Then suddenly the pilot appeared at the door, with a large parachute strapped securely on his back.

"Now don't you worry," he said. "I'm going for help."

◆

You really can't question her when she says she's only thirty-five years old. Anybody who sticks to the same story for ten years has to be telling the truth.

"Wouldn't it be neat to know the time and place that you were to die?" asked a frivolous teenage girl.

"What good would that be?" asked her boyfriend.

"I wouldn't show up," she said.

◆

A man in the mental institution was enrolled in the art class. This class was to help heal the patients.

A visitor came by and noticed the patient dabbling away on the canvas, with an absolutely dry brush.

The visitor, noticing the canvas was blank, said, "Friend, what is your picture?"

The patient said, "It's a picture of the Egyptians chasing the Jews across the Red Sea."

"Where is the sea?" he asked.

"Oh, that's rolled back to let the Israelites through," he answered.

"Where are the Egyptians?" he asked.

"Oh, they'll be along in a minute."

◆

Fortune-teller: "You'll be poor and unhappy until you are forty."

Client (hopefully): "Then what?"

Fortune-teller: "You'll get used to it."

Harry, one day, attended Sunday school where the class read together the parable of the Prodigal Son, and had a lesson about it.

"And what happened when the Prodigal Son returned?" asked the teacher when question time came.

"His father went to meet him and hurt himself," replied one of the class.

"Hurt himself?" said the teacher. "Wherever did you learn that?"

"From the Bible, sir," replied Harry. "It says his father ran to meet him and fell on his neck."

✦

A man trying to understand the nature of God asked:

"God, how long is a million years to you?"

And God said, "A million years is like a minute."

Then the man asked, "God, how much is a million dollars to you?"

And God said, "A million dollars is like a penny."

The man thought for a moment and asked, "God, will you give me a penny?"

And God said, "In a minute."

A Texan was always bragging about Texas being the biggest in everything, so his friends decided to get even with him.

So they put some knockout drops in his coffee. They put on him a white robe, and placed him in a coffin, in a graveyard by a freshly dug grave.

He awakened about sunrise, sat up, and looked at the golden sunrise.

He said, "Praise the Lord! It's resurrection morning and a Texan is the first one resurrected!"

◆

A high school class was holding its twenty-fifth reunion. Among them was a man named Bill, who was almost completely bald. Someone asked him: "Bill, have you realized any of the ambitions or desires you had as a boy?"

Quickly Bill responded: "I sure did. When my mother used to comb my hair or make me comb my hair, I often wished I didn't have any."

◆

A Texan was visiting Niagara Falls.

"I bet you haven't got anything like that in Texas," a local resident said, pointing to the falls.

The Texan, scratching his head, said, "No, but we have a plumber who can stop that leak!"

Funny Stuff

The committee of the small town decided to have a short program for Memorial Day services following the parade. They sent a letter to a well-known citizen that read: "You are hereby invited to be the speaker at the Memorial Day program. The program will include a talk by the mayor, a reading by a high school girl, your talk, and then the firing squad."

✦

A traveling man one night found himself obliged to remain in a small town because of a washout on the railroad. He turned to the waitress with: "This certainly looks like the Flood."

"The what?"

"The Flood. You have read about the Flood, and the Ark landing on Mount Ararat, surely."

"No, mister," she replied. "I ain't seen a paper for three weeks."

✦

An old man saw a boy struggling in the lake.

"What seems to be your trouble?" the old man called out.

"Help! Help! I can't swim!" screamed the boy.

"Well, Son, now is your chance to learn," the old man called back.

A well-dressed lady went to the airport with a dog kennel.

She said, "I want my dog on the plane first, and off the plane first in New York."

When the plane arrived and they took the kennel off the plane they discovered the dog was dead.

What are we going to do? they thought. Then one of the men said, "I saw a cute little dog that looks just like the dead dog. Let's get it and she'll never know the difference."

They brought the dog to the woman, and she said, "That's not my dog. My dog is dead."

A keen lover of rare books met an unbookish guy who had just thrown away an old Bible packed away for generations in the attic of his ancestral home.

"Somebody named Gutten-something had printed it," he said.

"Not Guttenberg!" gasped the book lover. "You've thrown away one of the very first books ever printed. One copy sold at an auction recently for over $400,000."

The other man, unmoved, said, "Oh, my copy wouldn't have brought a dime—some fellow named Martin Luther had scribbled notes all over it."

Funny Stuff

There was a fire in the middle of a group of apartment buildings. The fire department was called and one fire truck was blocks ahead of all the others getting to the fire. He drove at a dangerously high speed. He quickly put out the fire.

The mayor had a dinner for the fireman, and gave him a gift, and made a speech about how he had saved all the apartment building by getting there so fast and extinguishing the house fire.

When presenting him the key to the city, he said, "What can we give you for your great work?"

The fireman replied, "Brakes."

A farmer had an old mule that balked on him, and wouldn't move an inch.

He called the veterinarian and asked him to give the mule something to make him move.

The doctor gave him a special powder which he gave mules. Suddenly the mule started off like a rocket across the field. The farmer said, "Doc, what did that powder cost that you gave the mule?"

"Fifty cents," the doctor replied.

Very excitedly the farmer said, "Then you had better give me a dollar's worth, because I've got to catch that mule, you know."

Two solemn-minded fishermen went fishing one summer day in an old launch. For three hours neither of them moved a muscle. Then the one up forward became a bit restless.

"Confound it," grumbled his companion. "That's the second time you've shifted your feet in twenty minutes. Did you come out here to fish or practice dancing?"

◆

A United States pilot in Tokyo met a fellow who claimed he had been a kamikaze pilot in World War II. "But the war is over now," said the kamikaze pilot. "Let's be friends. My name is Chow Mein."

"But kamikaze flyers were suicide pilots," said the American. "If you had really been one, you'd be dead now."

The former kamikaze smiled wryly. "My name is Chicken Chow Mein."

◆

I have decided that the only way to get out of bed every morning with a big smile on your face is to go to bed at night with a coat hanger in your mouth.

Ribbing the Retired

Ribbing the Retired

An old couple from Texas took a trip to the East. The wife couldn't hear very well, and was doing all the driving.

They stopped for gas and the man at the old-fashioned gas pump said, "This is the fanciest car I have ever seen, what kind is it?" The husband told him it was a Mercedes.

The hard-of-hearing wife said, "What did he say?" The husband told her he wanted to know what kind of car they drove.

The man at the pump said, "Where are you folks from?" The husband told him they were from Cross Plaines, Texas.

The wife said, "What did he say?"

"He wanted to know where we were from," said the husband.

The man at the pump said, "Cross Plaines—why that's the town where I met a woman long ago, and she was the meanest woman I have ever met. Man, she was ornery. What a woman."

The wife said, "What did he say?"

The husband said, "He said he knew your sister."

A young doctor examined an old man. "And how do you feel?" the young doctor asked.

"Not so good," the old man sadly said. "My left leg is giving me fits, it hurts something awful!"

"Oh, don't you think that's just old age, my friend?"

"No," the old man said. "My right one is the same age as my left, and it don't hurt none!"

◆

An old man, ninety years of age, read in the newspaper that his country needed blood for blood transfusions very badly. He decided to help, so he went to the hospital and said, "I want to give some blood."

They put him on the table, and a needle in his arm. Afterward he was given a glass of orange juice.

"Oh, I feel great, better than ever. I think I'll just give some more right now."

"Sir," the doctor said, "we didn't take any of your blood, but we gave you a pint."

◆

"My eighty-five-year-old grandfather gets up early every morning to jog two miles."

"That's great! What's he do in the afternoon?"

"The last mile."

Ribbing the Retired

An old couple had a grandfather clock that struck each hour. Something went wrong with it one day, and it struck eight when it should have struck four. . .and four when it should have struck eight, and so on.

That night about eleven o'clock, it really went on a rampage and struck sixteen.

The old man jumped out of bed, shook his wife, and said, "Wake up, old lady, get up quick! It's later than it's ever been before!"

An old lady took a faded photograph of her late husband to a photographic studio. "Can you make a color portrait from this snapshot?" she asked.

"Yes, it's possible," said the photographer.

"And could you curl his mustache?" she asked. "And remove the wart from his nose?"

"Yes, it's possible," said the photographer.

"And could you take that hat off his head, so that his lovely black wavy hair shows?"

"Yes, it's possible, ma'am, but which side did he part his hair on?" the photographer inquired.

"Oh," said the little old lady, "I can't remember, but you'll find out when you take his hat off!"

An old man said to his wife, "Honey, you just don't hear me, I just don't think your hearing is good. So I'm going to test you. You go to the back of the room and I'll test you."

"Now, do you hear me?" There was no answer, so he moved very near her.

"Now, can you hear me?" Still no answer, so he said, "Honey, I asked you twice if you heard me, and you didn't answer me."

His wife said, "Three times I answered you, and you didn't hear me."

A man about eighty-five years old heard about some pills that could restore his youth so he bought a box.

The directions read, "Take one pill each day for thirty days." But he was impatient, so he took all thirty the first day at bedtime.

The next morning he didn't get up at his usual time. After a couple of hours, his family went into his bedroom and began to shake him, trying to wake him up.

Finally, he turned over, opened one eye, and yawned. Recognizing his family, he said, "Okay, okay, I'll get up for breakfast, but I'm not going to school today."

Ribbing the Retired

An advertising executive with a tobacco company came across a ninety-four-year-old man who had smoked four packs of cigarettes a day since he was twelve. The old-timer seemed to be in excellent health.

"We're getting ready to film some commercials," the ad man told the man. "I'll pay you $1,000 if you'll agree to let us put you in some of them."

"Sure," answered the old fellow. "When do you want me?"

"Be at the studio at nine o'clock tomorrow morning."

"No good," the smoker replied. "I don't stop coughing until noon."

✦

A newspaper interviewed a grizzled old man, sitting with his hands folded in his lap, behind his farmhouse.

"Sir, I'd like to know the secret of your long life," asked the reporter.

"I drink a gallon of whiskey, smoke fifty cigars, and go out dancing every day of my life," said the man.

"Remarkable!" said the reporter. "And exactly how old are you?"

"Twenty-seven," was the reply.

LIKE JOKES OR TRIVIA?

Then check out these great books from
Barbour Publishing!

*A Funny Thing Happened on My Way through
the Bible* by Brad Densmore
    A different twist on the traditional Bible
trivia book. Share it with family and friends!
    Paperback. $2.49

*500 Clean Jokes and Humorous Stories and
How to Tell Them* by Rusty Wright and Linda
Raney Wright
    Everything you need to improve your
"humor quotient"—all from a Christian
perspective.
    Paperback. $2.49

Church Challenge by Marvin Hinten
    Fascinating, and often funny, trivia tidbits
from nearly 2,000 years of church history.
    Paperback. $1.99

Fun Facts about the Bible by Robyn Martins
    Challenging and intriguing Bible trivia—
expect some of the answers to surprise you!
    Paperback. $2.49
